ARISE AND SHINE

Your Destiny Battle at the Gate of Faith.

By:

Kesha D. Dunigan

Copyright © 2025 by Kesha D. Dunigan

All rights reserved. No part of this publication may be reproduced, stored in a retrieval system, or transmitted in any manner without the prior written consent of the publisher or the author, except in the case of brief quotations with proper reference embodied in critical articles and reviews. All quotations remain the intellectual property of the originator. All use of quotations is done under the fair use copyright principle.

Scripture quotations marked KJV are from the King James Version of the Bible. Scripture quotations marked NLT are from the Holy Bible, New Living Translation. Visit the author's website, at keshadunigan.com and mmeaaruwkah.com

Cataloging-in-Publication Data is on file with the Library of Congress

Paperback ISBN: 979-8-89401-073-1

Hardback ISBN: 979-8-89401-093-9

E-book ISBN: 979-8-89401-074-8

ABSOLUTE AUTHOR PUBLISHING HOUSE

DEDICATION

I dedicate this book to the Glory of the Lord Jesus Christ, who has inspired me by His Holy patience and persistence in my desire to answer the call to be of service to the Kingdom. I pray that everyone who reads this book will open their hearts to his will and his ways.

To my daughter for being the voice of support, my first student and disciple in the word of Christ. I love you always and forever. Thank you sincerely!

To my departed mother and father, I am eternally grateful for the time we had together and all the lessons you passed on to me. I especially thank my mother for her ingenuity and uncommon faith. She believed that I would get here even when the odds were against me. She never lost her faith in what God can do!

And to every student that I've had the pleasure of working with, thank you for your commitment to the Lord and the courage that you display as you follow the word of God with fire.

May his name be eternally praised. Amen.

PREFACE

Life has been full of ups and downs, peaks and valleys, light and darkness, losses and gains. Only those who are steadfast in prayer and led by the Holy Spirit have been able to navigate their way out of the captivity and chaos that the devil has subjected many generations to. In my own journey, developing a prayer life with the Lord and understanding His principles is a lifetime commitment—one with both internal and external challenges.

I remember when I walked in a time of spiritual blindness and biblical deafness. That season posed many learning opportunities for me. Through them, I learned to hear God and truly know Him in this world full of masqueraders, the spiritually dead, and wicked deceivers.

During this journey, a man once asked me, *"Do you remember when you were younger, going to Sunday school, and your pastor would say people are inherently good?"* He then explained, *"Since you do not know the secrets or the hearts of men, how can we know they are good? I might not know the hearts of men, but what I do know is God gave you a beautiful heart. I don't have to know you to see that. You must do everything to keep the heart the Lord has given you and the love you have for Him and His children. Your heart, which came from the Highest God, is a prize the enemy would work diligently and strategically to take from you."*

In all transparency, I did not understand what he was saying to me then. But now I know he had given me the first lesson in what became the longest and most treacherous battle I've ever experienced. Don't get me wrong—I've faced many battles since, but that statement and what followed was the hardest because, up to that point, my faith had endured trials, but my heart had never been challenged like this.

The enemy spared no resources, and the attacks were relentless. This is why it's critical for your spiritual walk and relationship with the Lord to surround yourself with *real* believers—Bible-believing, faith-walking, fire-speaking, destiny-moving followers of the true Gospel of God. You cannot afford lukewarm company or circumstances when tested by the enemy. Believers must understand: the devil (the thief) comes to **steal** (your heart), **kill** (your faith), and **destroy** (your connection with God)—but Jesus came to give you **life and life more abundantly** (John 10:10).

It was around this time the real journey began. I received on-the-job training (OJT) in hearing from God and wearing the **full armor of God** (Ephesians 6:11–13), all while learning to wield the greatest weapon: discernment and **praying without ceasing**. In my most vulnerable and dangerous battles, I found the truth and light of God. Before His direction enlightened me, I was desperate for answers. I lost sleep worrying about attacks on my career, health, ministry, finances, relationships—even my relationship with God.

When you lack answers and haven't perfected your prayer life or maintained the fire of the Holy Spirit, you'll feast at *anyone's* spiritual table just to find peace—in waking life, dream life, *any* life. Failing to recognize the rotten fruit of these tables is tragic; it poisons your spirit, mind, and soul.

My dear friends and family, hear this: when worry and fear consume you, the enemy's arrows have already been activated. Like in the book of Job, once our focus shifts to setbacks, our hedge is broken. We forget the enemy outside is clawing to get in, and *everything* that once brought joy or fulfillment becomes a target.

Like many before me, I've experienced the **goodness of the Lord in the land of the living** (Psalm 27:13). I was careless and misinformed, like Job's friends. I assumed such challenges only came through sin—but I quickly learned I didn't know Scripture as well as I thought. The school of hard knocks became my classroom.

That's why I created this prayer book: for anyone under heavy warfare seeking a starting point to **claim authority over every hardship**. Declare this is your time to **arise and shine** (Isaiah 60:1)—far above the enemy's reach!

The book of **1 John 5:19 (KJV)** reveals that *"the whole world [around us] lies in the power of the wicked one"*—the devil, **who** is the overseer of the world. From Scripture: *"So the dragon was enraged with the woman, and he* *went off to wage war on the rest of her children (seed), those who keep and obey the commandments of God and have the testimony of Jesus [holding firmly to it and bearing witness to Him]"* (**Revelation 12:17 AMP**).

In this book, you'll find a step-by-step process to assist you—no matter where you are in your spiritual understanding. It will help perfect your prayer life as you wage war against the devil, overcome him, and possess what is rightfully yours.

Introduction

In the beginning, God created the heavens and the earth and everything therein. After God had created all these things, He created man in His own image and likeness so that man would have dominion over everything He created (Genesis 1:28). When the devil saw the glory God lavished on man (Psalm 8:4–8), he became jealous and rebelled against God, taking along with him one-third of the angels in heaven (Revelation 12:3–9) so that he could stand on his own and rule over everything God had created (Isaiah 14:13–14).

God placed man in a beautiful garden named Eden, which bore all things needed to live a successful and prosperous life food, shelter, mineral resources, and, greatest of all, the presence of God (Genesis 1:7–14).

But the devil, a cunning creature according to his name ("serpent"), hijacked from man the power to dominate what God had given him and made the children of God slaves through the sin of disobedience that man committed.

The fall of man came because of Adam's disobedience, and it **affected** the future of mankind, causing us to live in ignorance, hardship, suffering, death, and sickness due to the escalation of sin. The struggle for men and women today is doubled by a false or limited understanding of biblical instructions before departing from Earth (The Holy Bible).

But let us circle back to the Garden of Eden. If you study the text, one might ask: *Why did the serpent only approach Eve?* She was made from Adam's rib—and did he not live in the garden first? This should be obvious—he had no authority to engage with Adam. One might wonder if there was a hedge of protection over Adam, and indeed there was! It took the form of a direct instruction from his father and Creator, requiring just one thing from Adam: obedience. The Lord had told Adam, *"Do not eat from the forbidden fruit of the tree of knowledge"* (Genesis 3:1–7).

Something else stands out: The serpent used temptation to lure Eve exploiting her access, insight, and influence and then drew Adam outside his hedge of protection through sin. Was this a case of ignorance or carelessness?

We now know that the fall of man did things **to** man and **in** man. It stole man's possessions, his righteousness and innocence, subjected him to a cursed land, and most devastatingly destroyed the relationship between God and man, condemning humanity to separation and shame (Genesis 3:14–19).

But all glory to God, who made a way out from the beginning (Ephesians 1:5)! He gave Jesus Christ, His only begotten Son, as the ransom for man's sin, restoring us to our rightful position as in the beginning. This restored the power of dominion back to man so that we might regain access to eternal life and all possessions (John 3:16). Through this, the source of life flows from Jesus to everyone who believes in Him, granting them the power to overcome Satan, who has vowed to wage war against believers (Revelation 12:17), and to triumph over him.

To claim restoration and be redeemed from all that has occurred in our lives begins with salvation. Without reconciliation with God, it is impossible to recover your light and all that has been stolen, murdered, or destroyed by the devil and his evil kingdom.

I strongly believe God is set to use this prayer book to deliver you from the power of the devil, who has subjected the world to darkness and pain. God wants to grant you access to redeem the time and restore what has been lost or stolen from you. As you read this book, take in the prayers and follow the instructions provided.

Remember, it is not the hearer who will receive the blessing but those who obey the instructions (James 1:25; Joshua 1:8).

Table of Contents

Introduction viii

CHAPTER 1 .... *1*

Prayer Over Your Water & Oil 1

CHAPTER 2 .... *6*

The Believers Prayer 6

CHAPTER 3 .... *8*

Faith is Key to Battle 8

CHAPTER 4 .... *10*

The Seed of Faith Saves 10

CHAPTER 5 .... *16*

Faith of the Demonic Kind 16

CHAPTER 6 .... *32*

Faith in Mind, Body and Spirit 32

CHAPTER 7 .... *39*

Using Faith to Battle the Enemy 39

CHAPTER 8 .... *40*

Get Your Faith Weight Up 40

CHAPTER 9 .... *44*

Faith is the weapon for battle 44

CHAPTER 10 50
Faith Activation of Healing 50

CHAPTER 11 56
Faith to Activate the Finger of God 56

CHAPTER 12 67
Let us speak and pray 67

CHAPTER 13 71
Faith Must Stand Trail 71

CHAPTER 14 79
No Fear Permitted 79

CHAPTER 15 86
What Faith Can Do that No Man Can Not Do 86

CHAPTER 16 91
Activation of Great Faith 91

CHAPTER 17 93
Prayer of Praise and Thanksgiving 93

CHAPTER 18 95
My Time to Rise: Tested Faith 95

Closing Prayer 124

Faith Confession Prayer Glossary 126

CHAPTER 1

Prayer Over Your Water & Oil

As you study the prayers in this book, you may use the following prayer to bless your water and oil. The blessed water can be used for cleansing baths, face and hair washes, and even as drinking water. Likewise, the oil can serve as your personal anointing oil, which may be used in cleansing baths, for personal anointing, and for blessing areas around your home.

To create a focused and spiritually enriching experience, it is encouraged to prepare a quiet space for prayer. Having your Bible, a pen, and a notepad nearby is also beneficial, as it allows you to capture thoughts, insights, and revelations that may come to you during your reading and prayer time.

When preparing your prayer water, please use a clean glass or an unopened bottle of water. For your prayer oil, olive oil is the most commonly used base, but if that is unavailable, you may use any pure oil you have. If possible, avoid mixed oils or those containing fragrances or essential oils, as some ingredients may be unclean or sourced from impure origins. Using oils with unknown or unclean components could compromise the spiritual integrity of your blessed oil, rendering it ineffective or even detrimental to your spiritual walk.

Once your oil has been prayed over, you may use it as you see fit, including incorporating it into natural lotions or body washes. While reading this book, I encourage you to anoint yourself with your oil and keep your prayer water close by.

When anointing your home, it is recommended to start from the northern part of your home. This aligns with **Jeremiah 4:5–18**, which speaks of the enemy attacking from the north. By beginning in the north and moving throughout your space, you are spiritually fortifying your home against any forces that seek to disrupt your peace and blessings.

Now, once you have gathered your clean water and oil and have prepared your space, please proceed with the following prayer:

In the name of Jesus Christ, I am a beloved child of God. I believe in God. I believe in Jesus Christ, and I believe in the blessed Holy Spirit, who dwells inside of me. I believe in the unshakable and eternal power of the word of God. I believe that life and death are on my tongue. I believe that as I make this confession unto life with the power in my tongue, according to the words which the Lord has this day put in my mouth, I shall prosper.

It is written that Jesus Christ offered His blood as a drink and His flesh as bread, that whoever drinks and eats them shall not die forever. Now, with strong faith in my heart, I hold in my hand a cup containing the blood of the Lamb of God, and I drink it, that I may have eternal life. I receive unto myself the virtues, strength, power, might, and anointing in the blood. And I say: Let the blood quicken all that is dead within me. Let all sucked, sapped, and paralyzed spiritual milk and strength of my life be resurrected by the blood. Let the blood re-energize, revitalize, and reactivate all dead potentials and spiritual gifts within me.

Let the blood flush out of me all inherited or self-acquired evil deposits in my system. Let it purify my bloodstream. Let it make old things pass away in my life and transform everything to become new. Let the power in the blood cleanse my spiritual vision and wash my spiritual pipes, that I may receive from the Lord unhindered. **I eat with the heart of faith the flesh of Jesus, for it is written:** *"His flesh is bread indeed."* I eat it now so that I may also eat with Him in His glory. I eat the flesh of Jesus to receive new spiritual strength and vigor to put under subjection all works of the flesh. I paralyze the desires of my flesh and make it obedient to the laws of the Lord.

As I eat and drink the flesh and blood of my Lord Jesus Christ, I renew my covenant with Him. I receive the life therein, **for it is** written: ***"Life is in the blood."*** I possess the life and the Spirit of Christ in me. Amen.

Jeremiah found the word of God and ate it, and it became the joy of his heart. I have found the word of God, and now, like vitamin pills, I throw it into my mouth, chew it, and digest it. Let it produce within me the power to rejoice in the Holy Ghost, the power to be steadfast in following God, the power to walk circumspectly, the power of holy living, and the power of unashamed faithfulness in all circumstances.

The word of God is the Spirit, and it is life. It entered Ezekiel, and he was put back on his feet. Let the word of God raise up in me in every downtrodden area of my life. Let the word, like fire, purify me and restore any parts stolen or destroyed by the enemy. Let the word build me up and give me an inheritance among all sanctified brethren.

Let the joy of the Lord strengthen me. Let His right hand of righteousness upholds me. Let His countenance brightens my life. Let the horn of His salvation lift me out of the valley of life, and let His living anointing oil fall on me like the dew of Hermon and fill my life.

Lord, make me drunk with the blood of Jesus, and I shall be full of eternal life. Father Lord, **as it is written,** ***"Be strong in the Lord and in the power of His might."*** I ask that You be my might and strength all the days of my life. Gird me with Your strength, and let me not fall into the pit of my enemies, and I will praise You all the days of my life.

With my heart, I believe the word of God. With my mouth, I have confessed unto salvation and justification. **Oh Lord, let it be performed unto me as I have prayed, in Jesus Christ's only mighty name. Amen.**

CHAPTER 2

The Believers Prayer

Father, I come to You humbly in the name of **Jesus Christ**, whom I believe is my Lord and Savior. I give You all the glory and all the praise. I am thankful for Your wonder-working victory and dominion, established by Your only begotten Son, **Jesus Christ**—He who died on the cross of Calvary for me, conquered victory over death, entered the lowest parts of the earth, and took the keys of hell, death, and sin, nailing them to the cross of **Calvary. Therefore**, they have no dominion over me.

I ask for Your forgiveness and mercy for the sins of disobedience I have committed against You and any of Your children. I cover myself in the precious blood of the **Lamb of God** and set a hedge of fiery protection around me.

Father, I turn my life over to You to do as You will. I ask that You come into my life and make everything crooked straight. Fill me up with Your **Spirit**, O God of **Abraham, Isaac, and Jacob**. Take complete control over my every thought. Help me to walk in total victory, which You have provided for me.

I desire fellowship with You—that You reveal to me the things that grieve Your heart and enable the enemy to establish a case against me, giving him a foothold in any area of my life.

I decree and declare that You are the light and the stronghold of my life. Therefore, the weapons of my warfare are mighty and not carnal. I pull down every stronghold and cast down every vain imagination that exalts itself against the **Word and knowledge of God.**

I believe and decree that the anointing of the **Holy Spirit** breaks every yoke of captivity, slavery, blindness, deafness, and mindlessness.

Lord Jesus, you are my deliverer and my peace. **Therefore**, every weapon of darkness formed against me shall be broken. There will be no reconnection, re-establishment, or renewal of any ungodly covenant or demonic decree.

My faith has activated the fire of deliverance to rain down upon me—from the crown of my head to the soles of my feet—burning up every obstacle in the way of my **breakout and breakthrough**. Thank You, **Father**, for answered prayers, in **Jesus' name**.

I decree by the power of the **Almighty God**: As you prayerfully journey into this book, you shall rise and shine, for your light has come. All the keys to your possessions will be given unto you, in **Jesus' name. Amen!**

CHAPTER 3

Faith is Key to Battle

Faith is the assurance of things hoped for, the conviction of things not seen (*Hebrews 11:1*). There are four types of faith, and depending on your relationship and walk with the Highest God, you will need to pray fervently and stay consistent in your biblical studies. Through reading, you will begin to learn about the power, boldness, and authority of the Word of God and His impact on your assigned destiny.

Four Types of Faith & Scriptures:

1. **Faith That Saves** (*John 3:16*): God gave His only begotten Son on **Calvary** for our sins, and it is in the name of Jesus that we find all-around peace and victory.
2. **Faith Without Works Is Dead** (*James 2:17*): Spiritual fruits should be present. You need to see the fruit of the Spirit working in your life (*Galatians 5:22-26*).
3. **Demonic Faith** even the fallen angels' shudder at the name of Jesus (*James 2:19*): Every knee must bow to the precious name of the Lord Jesus Christ.
4. **Vain Faith** is believing without cause or without success (*Matthew 7:21-23; 1 Corinthians 15:14*): This happens when you

are not committed to what you believe, and your connection to the Word of God is weak in your heart.

CHAPTER 4

The Seed of Faith Saves

One might ask, *"What is the meaning of faith that saves?"* The most relevant passage to this question would be **James 2:14–26**, where James contrasts true saving faith with dead faith.

Let me clarify:

1. Understanding Faith That Saves

Faith that saves is a **genuine, active, and transformative** belief in Jesus Christ that produces obedience and good works as evidence of salvation. It is not merely intellectual assent but a deep, life-changing trust in God.

2. The Biblical Foundation for Saving Faith

There are two key perspectives on faith in the New Testament:

- **Paul** emphasizes *justification by faith apart from works* (**Romans 3:28; Ephesians 2:8–9**).
    - Paul teaches that salvation is a free gift received through faith, not earned by works.
    - Faith is trusting in Jesus' finished work on the cross, not human effort.

- **James** emphasizes that *faith without works is dead* (**James 2:14–26**).
  - James is not contradicting Paul but clarifying that true faith results in obedience.

3. John 2:16 and Its Connection

John 2:16 states:

"And He said to those who sold doves, 'Take these things away! Do not make My Father's house a house of trade!'"

While this verse does not directly discuss faith, it highlights Jesus' concern for **genuine worship** rather than empty religious rituals. This connects with the idea that true faith involves a transformed heart and actions that align with God's will. Just as Jesus cleansed the temple of corruption, saving faith cleanses your life, producing righteousness.

4. Key Elements of Saving Faith

- **Belief in Jesus Christ**: Acknowledging Jesus as Lord and Savior (**John 3:16; Romans 10:9**).
- **Repentance**: Turning from sin and surrendering to God (**Acts 3:19**).
- **Obedience to God's Word**: Living in alignment with His commands (**John 14:15**).
- **Fruit of the Spirit**: Evidence of transformation (**Galatians 5:22–23**).

5. A Warning Against False Faith

James 2:19 says:

"You believe that God is one; you do well. Even the demons believe—and shudder!"

This means that merely acknowledging God's existence is **not enough**. True saving faith moves beyond head knowledge to a heart commitment that results in a changed life.

Examples of Saving Faith in Scripture:

- **The thief on the cross (Luke 23:39–43)**: He trusted Jesus in his final moments and was promised paradise.
- **The Philippian jailer (Acts 16:30–31)**: He asked, *"What must I do to be saved?"* and was told, *"Believe in the Lord Jesus Christ, and you will be saved."*

Warning Against False Assurance:

- Faith is **more than knowledge**: Acknowledging Jesus exists is insufficient—you must surrender to Him.
- Faith is **more than emotion**: A temporary feeling does not equate to true salvation. It must lead to repentance and transformation.

Faith Without Works Explained

Faith Without Works Is Dead

The concept of "faith without works is dead" comes from **James 2:17**, which states:

"In the same way, faith by itself, if it is not accompanied by action, is dead." **(James 2:17, NIV)**

Explanation of James 2:17

In this verse, James emphasizes that true faith in God is not merely a mental acknowledgment or belief but is active and demonstrated through actions. This idea challenges the common misconception that faith is solely about having the right beliefs or understanding. James argues that if one's faith does not produce good works—such as acts of kindness, justice, mercy, and love—then it is dead and ineffective. Faith without tangible, godly actions does not reflect a true connection with Christ.

This teaching highlights the internal transformation in Christ that must be connected to external expressions. If you truly have faith, it will manifest in how you live—through how you treat others, respond to needs, and follow Christ's teachings daily.

Spiritual Fruits and the Fruit of the Spirit (Galatians 5:22-26)

Paul's letter to the Galatians further clarifies the relationship between faith and works:

"But the fruit of the Spirit is love, joy, peace, forbearance, kindness, goodness, faithfulness, gentleness and self-control. Against such things, there is no law. Those who belong to Christ Jesus have crucified the flesh with its passions and desires. Since we live by the Spirit, let us keep in step with the Spirit." (**Galatians 5:22-25, NIV**)

These qualities are not passive attitudes but active expressions of the Holy Spirit's work in your life. The fruit of the Spirit reveals Christ's transformative power within you. Genuine faith produces these fruits as evidence of your connection to Christ.

Connection Between Faith, Works, and Fruit

- **Faith as the Root**: Faith in Christ is the foundation of salvation (Ephesians 2:8-9) and the basis for all actions.
- **Works as the Fruit**: Works are the visible result of faith—not the cause of salvation, but its natural outcome. *"A tree is known by its fruit"* (**Matthew 7:16**).
- **Spiritual Fruit as Evidence**: The presence of love, patience, etc., confirms a believer's walk with the Spirit.
- **Living by the Spirit**: The fruit cannot be manufactured by human effort but flows from surrender to the Holy Spirit.

Key Points in Living Out True Faith

1. **Faith and Action Are Inseparable**: True faith leads to visible transformation (James 2:18).
2. **Spiritual Growth**: The fruits develop as you mature in Christ. We are called to *"keep in step with the Spirit"* (**Galatians 5:25**).
3. **Impact on Others**: Your works testify to God's love, drawing others to Christ.
4. **Ongoing Process**: Spiritual fruit grows gradually, reflecting God's character over time.

Examples of Faith with Works in Scripture

- **Abraham Offering Isaac (James 2:21-22)**: His faith was proven through obedience.
- **Rahab Helping the Spies (James 2:25)**: She acted on her faith, demonstrating its sincerity.

Warning Against Faith Without Works

- Faith without change is empty. Works do not save but confirm that faith is real.
- If spiritual fruit is absent, faith is not alive.

CHAPTER 5

Faith of the Demonic Kind

Understanding Demonic Faith in James 2:19

How can faith be demonic? Well, let's take a look at what I mean concerning this type of faith and why it is important to know the difference.

James 2:19 states: *"You believe that God is one; you do well. Even the demons believe and shudder!"*

This verse reveals a critical distinction between true saving faith and demonic faith (or false faith). James uses demons as an example to show that mere intellectual belief in God is not enough to save a person. True faith must be alive, active, and transformative.

1. What Is Demonic Faith?

Demonic faith is an intellectual acknowledgment of God's existence without true submission or obedience to Him. It is a kind of belief that recognizes the truth about God but does not lead to a transformed life.

Key Characteristics of Demonic Faith:

1. **Intellectual Knowledge Without Trust**: Demons believe in God, but they do not submit to Him.
2. **Fear Without Obedience**: They shudder in fear because they know His power and judgment but remain rebellious.
3. **Recognition Without Relationship**: They acknowledge Jesus' identity but do not have a relationship with Him.
4. **No Repentance or Transformation**: Unlike saving faith, demonic faith does not lead to a changed heart or good works.

This is the same kind of faith that many people today have—they acknowledge God's existence but live in disobedience, without repentance, and without true submission to Jesus Christ as Lord.

Having the fear of the Lord is essential to cultivating a genuine, non-demonic faith because it aligns our hearts with reverence, obedience, and submission to God's will. Unlike the fear that demons have—a fear rooted in terror and impending judgment—the fear of the Lord is a holy awe and deep respect for God's sovereignty, righteousness, and power.

How the Fear of the Lord Contributes to Non-Demonic Faith

1. True Faith Produces Obedience, Not Just Acknowledgment

- *James 2:19 says, "You believe that there is one God. Good! Even the demons believe and shudder."*
- This verse reveals that demons acknowledge God's existence and power, but their belief is not faith that leads to salvation. They fear His judgment but have no obedience or relationship with Him.
- Non-demonic faith, in contrast, is not just about recognizing God's power but living in submission and obedience to Him. The fear of the Lord leads to a transformed heart that seeks to honor Him, not just acknowledge Him from a distance.

2. **The Fear of the Lord Extends God's Mercy and Grace**

- *Psalm 103:17 – "But the mercy of the Lord is from everlasting to everlasting upon them that fear him, and his righteousness unto children's children."*
- God extends mercy and grace to those who fear Him because they walk in humility, repentance, and dependence on His guidance.
- A person who fears the Lord recognizes their need for God's forgiveness and actively pursues righteousness, unlike demons, who are irrevocably condemned and cannot receive mercy.

3. **The Fear of the Lord Leads to Wisdom and Spiritual Maturity**
    - *Proverbs 9:10 – "The fear of the Lord is the beginning of wisdom, and the knowledge of the Holy One is understanding."*
    - True faith matures through wisdom, discernment, and spiritual growth, all of which stem from a healthy fear of the Lord.
    - Unlike demons, who operate in deception, those who fear the Lord Walk in truth and divine revelation, allowing them to experience God's grace in full measure.

4. **Reverence vs. Terror: A Key Distinction**
    - Demons recognize Jesus' authority and fear His judgment (*Mark 1:24, "Have you come to destroy us?"*), but they do not worship or obey Him.
    - A believer who fears the Lord does not just fear punishment but seeks to honor God out of love, respect, and devotion.
    - This reverential fear draws believers closer to God, whereas demonic fear drives entities away from Him in torment and rebellion.

The fear of the Lord is what separates true faith from mere belief. It is not a crippling fear but a reverence that leads to obedience, wisdom, and an outpouring of God's mercy and grace. Demons may recognize

Jesus' power, but they lack submission, love, and redemption—all of which come through a true, godly fear that transforms and restores.

2. Biblical Examples of Demonic Faith

A. The Demons Recognized Jesus' Authority

- In *Mark 1:24*, a demon-possessed man cried out: *"What have you to do with us, Jesus of Nazareth? Have you come to destroy us? I know who you are the Holy One of God!"*
- The demon recognized Jesus' divine identity but did not submit to Him in faith. This proves that knowledge of Jesus does not equal salvation.

B. The Demons Bowed to Jesus but Were Not Saved

- In *Mark 5:6-7*, when Jesus confronted the man possessed by Legion, the demons fell at His feet and begged Him: *"What have you to do with me, Jesus, Son of the Highest God? I adjure you by God; do not torment me."*
    - They knew Jesus had absolute power over them.
    - They feared judgment but did not repent or submit.
    - They bowed in recognition of His power but remained His enemies.
- This mirrors *Philippians 2:10-11*, which declares that in the name of Jesus, every knee will bow but not everyone will bow in worship; some will bow in judgment.

3. The Difference Between Saving Faith and Demonic Faith

Demonic Faith	Saving Faith
Believes in God's existence	Trust in God for salvation
Acknowledges Jesus as Lord	Submits to Jesus as Lord
Knows Scripture but rejects obedience	Obeys God's Word with a transformed heart
Fears judgment	Rests in God's grace
No repentance	Repentance and a new life in Christ

4. Every Knee Must Bow: The Power of Jesus' Name

A. Every Creature Must Submit to Jesus' Authority

- **Philippians 2:9-11** states:

    "Therefore, God has highly exalted him and bestowed on him the name that is above every name, so that at the name of Jesus every knee should bow, in heaven and on earth and under the earth, and every tongue confess that Jesus Christ is Lord, to the glory of God the Father."

- This passage shows that:
    1. Jesus is exalted as Lord over all creation.
    2. Every being humans, angels, and demons must acknowledge His supremacy.
    3. The righteous will bow in worship, while the rebellious will bow in judgment.

B. The Authority of Jesus Over Demonic Forces

1. **Luke 10:17**: The disciples cast out demons in Jesus' name.
2. **Acts 16:18**: Paul cast out a demon by commanding it in the name of Jesus Christ.
3. **Matthew 8:29**: Demons begged Jesus, knowing He had the power to cast them into the abyss.

- The demons do not resist Jesus' power, but they also do not love or follow Him. This is the heart of demonic faith: **knowledge without obedience**.

5. The Danger of Having a Faith Like the Demons

Many people today believe in Jesus but do not obey Him. Jesus warned about this in **Matthew 7:21-23**:

"Not everyone who says to me, 'Lord, Lord,' will enter the kingdom of heaven, but the one who does the will of my Father who is in heaven."

Signs That Someone May Have Demonic Faith Instead of Saving Faith:

- They say they believe in Jesus but live in unrepentant sin.
- They acknowledge God's power but do not submit to His will.
- They attend church but do not have a personal relationship with Christ.
- They fear hell but do not seek holiness.
- Jesus wants more than lip service—He wants a heart surrendered to Him.

Examples of Demonic Faith in Scripture:

1. **Legion, the Demon-Possessed Man (Mark 5:6-13)**: The demons acknowledged Jesus but did not submit to Him.
2. **Satan's Knowledge of Scripture (Matthew 4:1-11)**: Satan quoted God's Word but twisted it for his own purposes.

Why This Faith Is Dangerous:

- Many people believe in God but do not surrender to Him.
- Belief without submission is still rebellion.
- True faith involves both **recognition** and **obedience**.
- **Vain Faith: Matthew 7:21-23; 1 Corinthians 15:14.**

Understanding Vain Faith: A Faith That Is Empty and Useless

Vain faith is a faith that lacks substance, commitment, and transformation. It is a superficial belief that does not result in salvation or true spiritual growth. The Bible warns about this kind of empty, ineffective faith. A faith that does not produce true obedience, commitment, or power (spiritual fire) in your life is vain and ineffective in your relationship with Christ Jesus.

Let's break down vain faith using **Matthew 7:21-23** and **1 Corinthians 15:14**, along with the connection between salvation, deliverance, and a willing heart.

1. Matthew 7:21-23: The Danger of False Faith

A. Jesus' Warning About Superficial Faith

- **Matthew 7:21-23** states:

    "Not everyone who says to me, 'Lord, Lord,' will enter the kingdom of heaven, but the one who does the will of my Father who is in heaven. On that day many will say to me, 'Lord, Lord, did we not prophesy in your name, and cast out demons in your name, and do many mighty works in your name? And then will I declare to them, 'I never knew you; depart from me, you workers of lawlessness.'"

B. What Does This Teach Us About Vain Faith?

- **Faith Without Obedience Is Useless**: Many claims to follow Jesus but do not do His will.
- **Religious Works Without Relationship Are Meaningless**: People can perform miracles, preach, or cast out demons and still be lost.

- **God Judges the Heart, Not Just Outward Actions**: Religious acts do not guarantee salvation if the heart is far from God.
- **Knowing About Jesus Is Not the Same as Knowing Jesus**: These people knew His name but did not have a personal relationship with Him.

This passage warns that vain faith is **faith in words only**; it does not bring true salvation because it lacks true commitment and transformation.

2. 1 Corinthians 15:14: Faith Without Resurrection Power Is Vain

A. The Importance of the Resurrection in True Faith

- **1 Corinthians 15:14** states:

    "And if Christ has not been raised, then our preaching is in vain, and your faith is in vain."

B. How This Connects to Vain Faith

- **If Jesus Did Not Rise from the Dead, Our Faith Is Empty**: Paul teaches that the power of our faith comes from the resurrection of Jesus Christ.
- **A Powerless Faith Is a Vain Faith**: If someone believes in Jesus but does not live in His resurrection power, their faith is weak and ineffective.

- **True Faith Produces Transformation**: If a person's faith does not result in new life, victory over sin, and spiritual growth, it is empty.

Just as a car without an engine is useless, faith without resurrection power is vain and powerless. It may look good from the outside, but it has no ability to take a person anywhere spiritually.

3. The Heart Must Be Willing: True Faith vs. Vain Faith

A. True Salvation and Deliverance Require a Willing Heart

- **Romans 10:10**:

  "For with the heart one believes and is justified, and with the mouth, one confesses and is saved."

- **Ezekiel 36:26**:

  "I will give you a new heart and put a new spirit in you; I will remove from you your heart of stone and give you a heart of flesh."

A person cannot experience true salvation or deliverance unless their heart is fully surrendered to God. A half-hearted commitment or a weak connection to **God's** Word results in vain faith.

B. Signs of a Weak Connection to God's Word

1. **Lack of Prayer and Bible Study**: No relationship with God.
2. **Inconsistent Obedience**: Saying one believes but does not follow Jesus.

3. **No Spiritual Growth**: Remaining the same year after year.
4. **Doubt and Compromise**: Easily shaken in faith.
5. **No Power in Spiritual Warfare**: Constant defeat against temptation and attacks of the enemy.

4. How to Move from Vain Faith to True Faith

A. Commitment to God's Word

- **Romans 12:2**:

  "Be transformed by the renewing of your mind **through** the Word of God."

- **Psalm 119:11**:

  "**I have** hidden Your Word in my heart that I might not sin against You."

B. Strengthen Your Relationship with Christ

- **John 15:5**:

  "Apart from Me, you can do nothing."

- **James 4:8**:

  "Draw near to God, and He will draw near to you."

C. Obedience and Action

- **James 2:26**:

  "Faith without works is dead."

- **Matthew 7:24-27**:

  "Everyone who hears these words of Mine and does them will be like a wise man who built his house on the rock."

D. Seeking Deliverance Through the Power of Christ

- **John 8:36**:

    "If the son sets you free, you will be free indeed."

- **Mark 16:17**:

    "And these signs will accompany those who believe: In My name, they will cast out demons..."

Deliverance comes when faith is not just words but **action**, commitment, and obedience to Jesus Christ.

Review Vain Faith vs. True Faith

Vain Faith	True Faith
• Says Lord, Lord, but does not obey	• Obeys Jesus from the heart
• Believes but has no transformation	• Produces fruit and growth
• Empty religious works	• Genuine relationship with Christ
• No power over sin or demons	• Victory through Christ's resurrection
• Weak connection to God's	• Strong foundation in

Word	Scripture
• No salvation or deliverance	• Freedom and eternal life
• Final Warning	

Characteristics of Vain Faith:

- **Professes Jesus Without Commitment:** "Not everyone who says to Me, 'Lord, Lord,' shall enter the kingdom of heaven, but he who does the will of My Father." *(Matthew 7:21)*
- **Trusts in Works Over Relationship:** "Many will say to Me in that day, 'Lord, Lord, have we not prophesied in Your name?'" *(Matthew 7:22)*
- **Denies the Resurrection Power:** "If Christ is not risen, then our preaching is empty, and your faith is also empty." *(1 Corinthians 15:14)*
- **This leads to Eternal Rejection:** "I never knew you; depart from Me, you who practice lawlessness!" *(Matthew 7:23)*

Examples of Vain Faith in Scripture:

- **The Pharisees (Matthew 23:27–28):** Outwardly religious but inwardly dead.
- **The Rich Young Ruler (Mark 10:17–22):** He desired eternal life but was unwilling to fully commit to Jesus.
- **Many So-Called Believers (John 6:66):** They followed Jesus until His teachings became difficult.

Why This Faith Is Dangerous:

Vain faith is dangerous because people may think they are saved while their hearts are far from God. True faith requires a willing heart, commitment, and obedience to **God's Word**.

1. It gives false assurance.
2. It focuses on religion, not relationships.
3. It ends in eternal rejection.

Comparison of These Four Types of Faith

Type of Faith	Belief in God	Obedience & Works	Leads to Salvation?	Example
Saving Faith	Yes	Yes, leads to transformation	Yes	John 3:16, Romans 10:9
Faith Without Works	Yes	No, lacks obedience	No, dead faith	James 2:17, Galatians 5:22-23
Demonic Faith	Yes	No, acknowledges, but rebels	No, leads to fear	James 2:19, Mark 5:6-13

Vain Faith	Yes	No, religious but without commitment	No, leads to rejection	Matthew 7:21-23, 1 Corinthians 15:14

Final Reflection: What Type of Faith Do You Have?

1. Are you truly saved, or do you just know about God?
2. Does your faith produce good works and spiritual fruit?
3. Is your faith just intellectual, or is it transforming your life?
4. Are you truly surrendered to Jesus, or are you just going through religious motions?

If your faith is not aligned with saving faith, **now** is the time to repent, commit fully to Christ, and allow Him to work in you. True faith is living and active and produces fruit for the glory of God.

CHAPTER 6

Faith in Mind, Body and Spirit

Faith is the foundation of a strong relationship with our Creator and His only begotten Son, Christ Jesus, but it must be built, strengthened, and guarded with holy anger to avoid deception and confusion. Many believers struggle with doubt, spiritual attacks, and false teachings because their faith is not deeply rooted. This study will focus on how to strengthen your faith in mind, spirit, and heart so that you remain steadfast in the truth.

1. Strengthening Your Mind: Renewing Your Thinking in Christ

The mind is a battlefield where deception begins. To avoid confusion, your mind must be transformed and guarded by the truth of **God's Word**.

A. Renew Your Mind Daily

- **Romans 12:2**: "Do not be conformed to this world, but be transformed by the renewal of your mind, that by testing you may discern what is the will of God, what is good and acceptable and perfect."

The world constantly bombards us with false ideologies, fears, and lies. If we do not renew our minds with Scripture, deception will creep in.

Daily Study: Meditate on one Scripture daily and reflect on how it applies to your life.

B. Take Every Thought Captive

- **2 Corinthians 10:4-5:** "We destroy arguments and every lofty opinion raised against the knowledge of God, and take every thought captive to obey Christ."

Identify thoughts that contradict **God's Word** (fear, doubt, lies). Replace them with truth.

C. Be Aware of False Teachings

- **Colossians 2:8:** "See to it that no one takes you captive by philosophy and empty deceit, according to human tradition, according to the elemental spirits of the world, and not according to Christ."

Many believers fall into confusion because they follow man-made doctrines, family traditions, or church traditions. Much of what we've heard was taught by man instead of **biblical truth**.

1. **Mark 7:7-9**: Jesus rebukes the Pharisees for elevating human traditions above God's law.
2. **Matthew 15:3-20**: Jesus challenges the Pharisees for breaking God's commands in favor of their traditions (vv. 3–6), then explains that true defilement comes from the heart, not external factors.

3. **Test Everything**: Before believing a teaching, compare it with **God's Word** (**Acts 17:11**).

Key Lessons:

1. Religious traditions must not override **God's Word**.
2. True worship comes from the heart, not rituals.
3. Sin originates from within (thoughts, words, and actions), not external factors.

D. Develop Discernment

- **Hebrews 5:14**: "But solid food is for the mature, for those who have their powers of discernment trained by constant practice to distinguish good from evil."

Discernment comes from constant study, prayer, and **testing of the spirits (1 John 4:1)**.

2. Strengthening Your Spirit: Walking in Power and Authority

The spirit is where faith becomes active and powerful. If your spirit is weak, you will struggle against attacks and deception.

A. Pray in the Spirit

• **Ephesians 6:18**: "Praying at all times in the Spirit, with all prayer and supplication."

Prayer connects you to God's presence and strengthens your inner being.

B. Fasting for Spiritual Breakthrough

- **Isaiah 58:6:** *"Is not this the fast that I choose: to lose the bonds of wickedness, to undo the straps of the yoke, to let the oppressed go free, and to break every yoke?"* Fasting breaks spiritual strongholds and helps believers hear God more clearly.

C. Walk in the Power of the Holy Spirit

- **Acts 1:8:** *"But you will receive power when the Holy Spirit has come upon you, and you will be my witnesses."* The Holy Spirit gives discernment, boldness, and spiritual gifts to overcome deception.

D. Worship as a Weapon

- **Psalm 22:3**: *"God inhabits the praises of His people."* Worship shifts your focus from problems to God's power.

3. Strengthening Your Heart: Developing Deep Love and Trust in God

The heart is the seat of faith. If it is weak or divided, confusion will take root.

A. Guard Your Heart Against Doubt and Fear

- **Proverbs 4:23**: *"Above all else, guard your heart, for everything you do flows from it."* Protect your heart by avoiding negative influences and feeding it with faith-filled truths.

B. Cultivate a Deep Love for God

• **Matthew 22:37**: *"Love the Lord your God with all your heart, soul, and mind."*

A strong faith is built on love, not just knowledge.

C. Obedience Strengthens Faith

• **James 1:22**: *"But be doers of the word, and not hearers only, deceiving yourselves."*

Faith grows when we live out what we believe.

D. Endurance Through Trials

• **James 1:3-4**: *"For you know that the testing of your faith produces steadfastness."*

Trials strengthen our faith and deepen our trust in God.

4. How to Recognize and Avoid Deception

Deception often comes in subtle ways. Here's how to recognize and resist it:

A. Know the Voice of the Good Shepherd

• **John 10:27**: *"My sheep hear my voice, and I know them, and they follow me."*

A strong relationship with Christ helps you distinguish His voice from deception.

B. Be Rooted in Scripture

- **Matthew 4:4**: *"Jesus defeated Satan by saying, 'It is written.'"* The Word of God is the weapon against lies.

C. Be Watchful and Stay in the Community

- **1 Peter 5:8**: *"Be sober-minded; be watchful. Your adversary, the devil, prowls around like a roaring lion, seeking someone to devour."* Spiritual isolation leads to deception; stay connected to strong believers.

1. Practical Steps to Strengthen Your Faith Daily

Action	Scripture	Why It Helps
Daily Bible Reading	Psalm 119:105	Guides your steps with the truth.
Prayer and Worship	1 Thessalonians 5:16-18	Builds spiritual intimacy with God.
Fasting	Matthew 6:16-18	Breaks spiritual chains and strengthens discipline.
Community and Fellowship	Hebrews 10:25	Protects against deception and discouragement.

Serving Others	Matthew 25:40	Strengthens faith through action.
Speaking God's Promises	2 Corinthians 4:13	Declares victory and builds boldness.

Prayer for Strengthened Faith

Lord, strengthen my mind to know Your truth, strengthen my spirit to walk in Your power, and prepare my heart to trust in You fully. Let my faith be unshakable so I am never deceived. In Jesus name, Amen.

CHAPTER 7

Using Faith to Battle the Enemy

The only **criterion** to work with God and manifest His power over the power of evil is **faith**. This is because *"without faith, it is impossible to please God"* (**Hebrews 11:6**), and if you do not, please God, you cannot manifest His power over the kingdoms of darkness.

When it comes to spiritual battles, warfare, and **reclaiming** your possessions, remember that one of the most vital parts of the believer's armor is faith. With this armor, **your faith** will shine so brightly that it will terrify all the agents of darkness and free those held captive.

Note: We can only wield the armor of God through faith (**Ephesians 6:11**). When the enemy attacks, the *"shield of faith"* (**Ephesians 6:16**) is your divine protection.

In **Hebrews 11:32–34**, Gideon, Samson, David, and others **achieved** great victories through faith, overcoming enemy powers and kingdoms that rose against Israel. **Today**, God still calls His people to rise in faith, stand firm in battle, and resist the attacks of the enemy.

CHAPTER 8

Get Your Faith Weight Up

David said, "Thou comets to me with a sword, and with a spear, and with a shield: but I come to thee in the name of the Lord of hosts, the God of the armies of Israel, whom thou hast defied" (1 Samuel 17:45, KJV).

David's story exemplifies a spirit of faith, trust, and boldness in God, shaped by his experiences as a shepherd and his deep relationship with the Lord. His faith was not a sudden reaction to Goliath's challenge but the result of a life built on trust, responsibility, and reliance on God's protection and provision.

1. David's Spirit of Faith as a Shepherd

As a shepherd, David faced constant challenges, such as protecting his flock from predators like lions and bears. These experiences built:

- **Courage**: Shepherding required him to confront dangerous animals rather than flee, knowing the sheep's survival depended on his actions.
- **Dependence on God**: In moments of danger, David relied on God for strength, wisdom, and protection. His victories over predators deepened his trust in God's power.

- **Leadership**: David learned to prioritize the flock's well-being over his safety, cultivating responsibility and selflessness.

These traits formed the foundation of his faith, giving him confidence that the God who delivered him in the past would do so again.

2. Boldness in Confronting Goliath

David's confrontation with Goliath reveals his unwavering trust in God:

- **Defending God's Honor**: David was offended by Goliath's mockery of Israel and God. His response reflects a heart aligned with God's purposes:
    - *"Who is this uncircumcised Philistine, that he should defy the armies of the living God?"* (1 Samuel 17:26). This highlights David's belief that God's power surpasses any earthly threat.
- **Confidence in God's Deliverance**: David's declaration to Saul roots his faith in past experiences:
    - *"The Lord that delivered me out of the paw of the lion, and out of the paw of the bear, he will deliver me out of the hand of this Philistine"* (1 Samuel 17:37).
- **Bold Action**: While Israel's army trembled, David stepped forward, declaring:
    - *"For the battle is the Lord's, and he will give you into our hands"* (1 Samuel 17:47).

3. Tension with His Brothers

When David questioned why Goliath was allowed to insult God's army, his brother Eliab reacted with anger (1 Samuel 17:28). This tension mirrors the resistance faced by those who walk in faith:

- **Misunderstood Boldness**: Eliab accused David of arrogance, failing to see his heart for God's honor.
- **Persistence in Faith**: David refused to back down, prioritizing God's purposes over human approval.

4. Faith and Leadership

David's faith and leadership were inseparable:

- **Protecting the Vulnerable**: As a shepherd and future king, he defended the weak.
- **Trusting God's Power**: He rejected Saul's armor, declaring victory through God alone.
- **Inspiring Others**: His faith rallied Israel's army to victory after Goliath's fall.

Note: In the story of David and Goliath, Goliath knew the essence of physical armor but failed to understand the place of spiritual armor. The book of **2 Corinthians 10:3** reveals that though we walk in the flesh, the weapons of our warfare are not carnal. Going into battle against David, Goliath did not understand how vulnerable he was to David's faith.

CHAPTER 9

Faith is the weapon for battle

Faith is a critical component of our spiritual armor, serving as both a shield and a source of strength in our daily battles. In **2 Corinthians 10:3**, we are reminded that though we walk in the flesh, our warfare is not of the flesh but is spiritual, requiring divine power to overcome. This verse highlights the importance of relying on faith to engage in spiritual warfare, trusting in God's strength rather than our own. **Romans 10:17** reinforces this by teaching that faith comes from hearing and hearing through the word of Christ. This underscores the necessity of grounding ourselves in Scripture, allowing it to build and fortify our faith. By understanding and applying these truths, we can effectively stand firm against the spiritual challenges we face, fully equipped with the armor of God.

Memory Scripture Verse:

Romans 10:17 says, *"So then faith comes by hearing, and hearing by the word of God."* Believers must give themselves to hearing the word of God for faith to be built up in them for manifestation. Faith is the action we take in response to what we have received from the word of God. It is more than just decreeing and believing in our hearts. Faith takes steps, and the word of God activates movement within the spirit man in response to what God has said.

Prayer Points to Activate Faith:

(Note: Bible verses remain untouched; only grammar/punctuation fixes outside Scripture.)

1. Thank You, Jesus, for filling me with Your Spirit and causing me to do exploits by Your mighty power in me. Thank You, marvelous God.
2. Lord, help **me** to give **myself** time to study and learn Your word. Let my faith increase by hearing Your words. Mighty God, help me not **to** be distracted from hearing the word and putting it to work in my life.
3. Lord, by faith, I enter Your arsenal and activate the heavenly weapons that I need to utterly defeat my enemies.
4. Lord, strengthen my faith to work with You and make me strong to overcome the temptations of the devil whenever he comes **near**, in Jesus' name.
5. I come against household enemies, and I put an end to their operations over my life and destiny, in Jesus' name.
6. By faith, I run through a troop and leap over every **hindering** wall of the enemy **that seeks to** hamper my progress. I take action according to the word of God.

7. Heavenly Father, thank You for the power of Your word. I pray that as I hear and meditate on Your word daily, my faith will grow strong. Let it move beyond belief into action, in Jesus' mighty name.
8. I declare that my steps **are** aligned with Your will, and I will act boldly in response to Your promises. In Jesus' name, Amen.
9. Lord, I believe Your word is alive and powerful. As I hear Your word, may my faith be activated to move mountains in the name of Jesus.
10. O Lord, teach me to take bold steps of faith, knowing that You are with me. Strengthen my spirit to respond to Your word with unwavering trust and action, in Jesus' name. Amen.
11. Father, I ask for an open heart to receive Your Word. Let Your words dwell richly within me. In Jesus' mighty name, Amen.
12. Let my faith grow each day and empower me to take practical steps that honor You. In Jesus' name, Amen.
13. God of wisdom, help me cultivate a heart that listens attentively to Your Word. Let every message I hear deepen my faith and stir me to action in Jesus' mighty name.
14. O Lord, I pray that Your Word will ignite a movement in my spirit, compelling me to act according to Your will, in Jesus' name. Amen.
15. Lord, I ask that as I receive Your Word, it will produce results in my life.

16. Let the faith that rises within me be more than words; let it be evidenced by my actions.
17. Show me the steps I need to take to see Your promises manifest. I trust you to lead me in this journey, in Jesus' name. Amen.
18. Father, I thank You for the gift of faith.
19. As I hear Your Word, fill me with boldness to take steps in faith, even when I don't see the full picture, in Jesus' mighty name.
20. O Lord, may Your Word stir courage in me to step out in obedience. I trust that You are guiding me every step of the way, in Jesus' name. Amen.
21. Lord, I know that faith is more than just hearing Your Word; it is acting upon it. Teach me how to move in faith with every word You speak to me.
22. O God of Elijah, help me step out of my comfort zone and walk in alignment with what You have called me to do, in Jesus' name. Amen.
23. God, grant me understanding as I listen to Your Word. I pray that faith will rise in my heart as I hear it and wisdom will guide my actions.
24. May I not just hear but apply Your Word in practical ways that bring glory to Your name, in Jesus' name. Amen.
25. Father, I commit to hearing Your Word consistently, for I know that faith grows by hearing. Help me grow in faith each

day as I listen to Your Word. Strengthen me to take action in faith, trusting that You will fulfill every promise You have made in Jesus' name. Amen.

26. Lord, as I hear Your Word, help me walk in obedience.
27. May my faith not be passive but active, moving me to act according to Your will.
28. Empower me to follow through on every instruction You give me, knowing that You are faithful to complete the work You began. In Jesus' name, Amen.
29. Heavenly Father, I pray for confidence in Your Word. As I hear the promises in Scripture, let faith arise in me to believe that You will do exactly what You say.
30. Help me take steps of faith with boldness, trusting that You will guide me and bring Your promises to pass. In Jesus' name, Amen.
31. Lord, I know that faith overcomes doubt and fear. As I hear Your Word, may it replace every doubt with certainty in Your goodness.
32. Teach me to respond to Your Word with trust, and let that faith drive me to take action, knowing that You will make a way. In Jesus' name, Amen.
33. Father, I come before You with a heart ready to receive. As I hear Your Word, let my faith grow in anticipation of the promises You have for me.

34. May my faith be seen in my actions as I take steps toward the fulfillment of Your Word in my life. In Jesus' name, Amen.

35. O Lord, Your Word strengthens and sustains me. As I hear it, let it help me persevere in faith. Even when challenges arise, let the faith I have in Your Word compel me to take action. I know that You are with me and will bring about Your good purpose in my life. In Jesus' name, Amen.

36. Father, Your Word declares that we are victorious in Christ. As I hear Your Word, let it activate a faith that moves me forward into victory.

37. Teach me to take courageous steps of faith, trusting that You have already won the battle. May my life reflect the power of Your Word. In Jesus' mighty name, Amen.

CHAPTER 10

Faith Activation of Healing

Now, let me show you a powerful example in the Scriptures. Turn to *2 Kings 2:19-22* with the eyes of childlike faith—the same kind of faith you use every day when you trust without question that food will be delivered, a ride will arrive, or that a product will be shipped to you from companies that may not share your beliefs. Apply that same unshakable, blind faith while reading, and you will surely experience your breakthrough!

"Now the men of the city said to Elisha, 'Behold, the situation of this city is pleasant, as my lord sees, but the water is bad, and the land is unfruitful.' He said, 'Bring me a new bowl and put salt in it.' So, they brought it to him. Then he went to the spring of water, threw salt in it, and said, 'Thus says the Lord: I have healed this water; from now on, neither death nor miscarriage shall come from it.' So, the water has been healed to this day, according to the words that Elisha spoke."
(*2 Kings 2:19-22*)

There are many things happening in the Scripture above that will change your life. Let us give thanks to the glory of God for His divine revelations and His blessings of understanding.

2 Kings 2:19-22 describes an event that occurred shortly after the prophet Elijah was taken up to heaven, and Elisha, his successor, began his prophetic ministry. These verses are noted for the miracle performed by Elisha, but they also reveal important lessons about God's power, the role of a prophet, and the faithfulness of God to His people.

In the passage above, the healing of the water in the city of Jericho by Elisha offers a profound example of faith in God's power to heal and restore. Elisha's actions, grounded in his complete trust in God, reflect both his role as a prophet and his deep faith in God's ability to transform seemingly hopeless situations. Here's a deeper look at how Elisha's faith is demonstrated:

1. Elisha's Faith in God's Authority Over Creation

When Elisha is approached by the people of Jericho, they present him with a practical problem: the water is contaminated, and as a result, the land is unproductive. The people acknowledge that the situation is beyond human solutions—they cannot fix the problem on their own.

Elisha's response reveals his faith in God's ability to intervene in the natural world. Rather than relying on conventional methods, Elisha instructs the people to bring a new bowl and salt—tools that may seem insignificant in addressing such a serious problem. Yet, Elisha knows that God's power can heal what appears to be an impossible situation. By using a new bowl and salt, Elisha demonstrates that God has complete control over creation and His power can bring about transformation in the physical world.

This shows that Elisha's faith is not limited by human understanding or limitations. He trusts that God's power is sufficient to heal the water and restore the land, even though the solution might not make sense to those around him.

2. Elisha's Obedience to God's Guidance

Elisha doesn't act on his own ideas but follows God's instructions faithfully. After the people bring the bowl and salt, Elisha goes to the spring and throws the salt into it, declaring that God has healed the water. This act is a clear sign that Elisha is following God's guidance in how to heal the water, not just acting out of his own initiative.

Elisha's obedience reveals that he fully trusts God's plan and methods, even if they might seem unconventional. His faith is expressed not only in what he believes God can do but also in his willingness to obey the specific instructions given to him.

3. Elisha's Faith in God's Word

Elisha declares God's Word over the situation: *"This is what the Lord says: I have healed this water. Never again will it cause death or make the land unproductive"* (2 Kings 2:21). By speaking God's Word, Elisha shows his complete faith in the truth and power of God's promises. Elisha does not rely on his own strength or understanding but declares the healing through God's authority.

The declaration of God's healing over the water is a prophetic act that demonstrates Elisha's belief in the power of God's Word. He believes that God's spoken Word has the authority to deliver and change the condition of the water, transforming it from being harmful and unproductive to life-giving and fertile. This act reflects a deep faith that God can and will fulfill His promises.

4. The Outcome: Confirmation of Faith

In verse 22, the healing of the water is confirmed: *"And the water has remained pure to this day, according to the word Elisha had spoken."* The fact that the water remains purified demonstrates that God honored Elisha's faith and obedience. Elisha's faith in God's power was not in vain God responded by confirming that His Word, spoken through Elisha, was effective. The water remained pure, and the land became productive, which was a clear sign that Elisha's faith in God's healing power was not misplaced.

5. The Symbolism of Salt

The use of salt in the healing of the water also reflects faith in the symbolic power of God's covenant. Salt was used in the Old Testament as a symbol of preservation and covenant (*Leviticus 2:13; Numbers 18:19*). By using salt, Elisha demonstrates that God's covenant with His people is not only one of promise but also of preservation. Through this act, Elisha shows his belief that God's covenant extends to the land and the people, bringing deliverance, restoration, and healing.

Lessons from Elisha's Faith in God's Healing Power

1. **Faith in God's Ability to Heal**: Elisha demonstrates that faith is not just believing that God *can* heal but acting in obedience to what He instructs. His faith in God's power to restore the water is evident not only in his words but in his actions.
2. **Complete Dependence on God**: Elisha's reliance on God, rather than human wisdom or conventional methods, shows that faith requires dependence on God's authority and provision. God doesn't need our help or understanding to bring about healing; all that is needed is our faith in action and obedience.
3. **God's Word Is Powerful**: Elisha's declaration that God has healed the water reveals that God's Word is powerful and effective. This reminds us that when God speaks, His Word brings transformation. We can have faith that God's promises will be fulfilled in our lives, just as His Word healed the water.
4. **God Heals and Restores**: The miracle shows that God cares about both physical and spiritual healing. The purification of the water symbolizes God's broader healing—His desire to

restore both creation and His people to wholeness. Nothing is too difficult for Him to restore.

5. **Obedience as an Expression of Faith**: Elisha's actions in throwing the salt into the water are an act of obedience that flows from his faith. True faith is not passive; it involves action in accordance with God's instructions. Elisha didn't question the method or hesitate—he immediately obeyed.

CHAPTER 11

Faith to Activate the Finger of God

Scripture Reading: Luke 11:20 *"If I cast out demons with the finger of God, surely the kingdom of God has come upon you."*

The Lord has given us divine instructions, reminding us that *how we begin is how we finish.* I speak to you today with unwavering, unshakable faith, with the fire of Elijah and the faith-confidence of Elisha, declaring that the finger of God is real. As you read this, I assure you that something is happening in the spiritual realm; your situation is shifting, and a breakthrough is manifesting in your life. With Christ Jesus, all things are possible.

It does not matter who you are, where you are, or what has happened. The finger of God can intervene at any moment, regardless of your circumstances. He can locate you anywhere, using anyone, any place, and any point of contact to pour out His anointing upon you. His power is limitless and more than enough to deliver you from whatever has bound you and stolen your peace.

What Is the Finger of God?

The phrase *"the finger of God"* in the Bible carries a deep and profound meaning signifying God's direct and powerful intervention in human affairs. It points to His sovereign authority, His ability to act in the world, and His power over all things, including people, circumstances, and forces of nature. This phrase appears in four key places in Scripture, each highlighting God's unparalleled power in situations that seem impossible.

Exodus 8:19

"This is the finger of God."

This verse occurs during the plagues of Egypt, when Moses and Aaron, by God's command, brought plagues upon Egypt to compel Pharaoh to release the Israelites. Pharaoh's magicians, who had initially replicated some signs, failed to duplicate the plague of gnats. They exclaimed:

"Then the magicians said to Pharaoh, 'This is the finger of God.' But Pharaoh's heart was hardened, and he would not listen to them, as the Lord had said." (Exodus 8:19, NIV)

The Magicians' Recognition of Divine Power

The magician's experts in Egyptian sorcery acknowledged that Moses' power came from a divine source beyond human capability. Their declaration confirms that God's intervention cannot be mimicked or thwarted by human means.

Symbolism of the "Finger of God"

1. **Divine Power and Authority**: Represents God's absolute control over creation, like a king's decree.
2. **Direct Intervention**: Shows God's active involvement in human affairs (e.g., the plagues).
3. **Immanent Presence**: Emphasizes God's nearness—His "finger" touches and directs history.
4. **Unmatched Power**: No human force can rival God's authority (Exodus 8:19 proves this).

Pharaoh's Hardened Heart

Despite the magicians' admission, Pharaoh's heart remained hardened. This reveals a critical truth: God sometimes permits stubbornness to fulfill His greater purpose (Romans 9:17). The hardening was not arbitrary but part of God's plan to display His glory and liberate Israel.

Moses and Pharaoh's Royal Family

Moses, raised as Pharaoh's grandson (Exodus 2:10), had to sever ties with Egypt to lead Israel. God's hardening of Pharaoh's heart also refined Moses' resolve, aligning him fully with God's mission.

Theological Implications

This narrative challenges us to consider the following:

- God's sovereignty over human choices.
- How divine justice and mercy intersect.

- Our response to God's call—unlike Pharaoh, will we yield?

God's Glory Revealed Through Hardening Hearts

The idea of God hardening hearts is not unique to Pharaoh. Throughout Scripture, we see instances where God uses difficult situations, including the hardening of hearts, to ultimately bring glory to Himself. The unyielding demonstration of God's use of hard hearts in His divine plan speaks to His sovereignty over every aspect of life—nothing is beyond His power or His ability to use for His greater purpose.

- In **Romans 1:24–28**, we see that God sometimes gives people over to their sinful desires and hardens their hearts, allowing them to follow their own rebellious path. This is not an arbitrary act but one that serves the broader purpose of making clear the justice and sovereignty of God.
- In **Isaiah 6:9–10**, God instructs the prophet to speak to a people whose hearts will be hardened. This is part of God's judgment upon Israel's unfaithfulness and serves as a means for His glory to be displayed in the midst of judgment.

The Ultimate Display of God's Power: Who Can Challenge Him?

As we reflect on the "finger of God" and the hardening of Pharaoh's heart, we are reminded that God is sovereign. He is the King of Kings, the Lord of Lords, the Alpha and the Omega. No one can challenge

His authority or power. The question arises: *"Who can stand before Him and challenge Him to battle? And win?"*

This rhetorical question underscores that no one can oppose God's sovereign will and prevail. In **Isaiah 45:9**, God declares:

"Woe to those who quarrel with their Maker, those who are nothing but potsherds among the potsherds on the ground. Does the clay say to the potter, 'What are you making?' Does your work say, 'The potter has no hands'?" (**Isaiah 45:9, NIV**) God's sovereignty over all creation means He is never in competition with anyone. Pharaoh, despite his position as ruler of the most powerful nation of that era, was nothing before God's infinite power. God used Pharaoh's stubbornness to demonstrate His might, ultimately leading to the deliverance of the Israelites and the proclamation of His glory across the earth.

There are six actions I want to share with you that the activation of the finger of God can do. When you act in obedience, see through the eyes of faith and walk according to his will and precepts.

1. Understanding the Finger of God

The "finger of God" symbolizes his power and authority in the Bible. It represents God's direct intervention in human affairs. Often in situations that seem impossible and generational. Let us muse through *Exodus 8:19 - "Then the magicians said to Pharaoh, 'This is the finger of God.'*

But Pharaoh's heart was hardened, and he would not listen to them, as the LORD had said."

The Lord displayed His power of divine intervention over all things—even to the hardening of Pharaoh's heart. Sometimes, the hearts of the people, places, and things must be hardened to acknowledge the greatness of our creator. So, you and whoever is involved will have no doubt who the author and the finisher of all things good for thee is. He is the king of kings and lord of lords, the alpha and the omega. Who can stand before him and challenge him to battle? And win?

The Finger of God in Deliverance

God's finger delivers his people from bondage and oppression. It is through his power that chains are broken and captives are set free. Luke 11:20 - "But if I drive out demons by the finger of God, then the kingdom of God has come upon you."

The Lord will deliver you out of every situation and circumstance and relocate you on that path of righteousness.

The Finger of God in Judgment

The finger of God can also bring judgment upon the wicked and those who oppose his will. It is a reminder that God is just and will act against unrighteousness.

Exodus 31:18* - "When the Lord finished speaking to Moses on Mount Sinai, he gave him the two tablets of the covenant law, the tablets of stone inscribed by the finger of God."

This verse marks a significant moment in biblical history. After God had given Moses detailed instructions on the laws and the construction of the Tabernacle, He personally gave Moses two stone tablets containing the Ten Commandments. These tablets were unique because they were written by the very finger of God, signifying divine authority and permanence.

Key Takeaways:

1. Divine Origin "The commandments were not just spoken but physically inscribed by God Himself, emphasizing their unchangeable nature.

2. Mount Sinai "This moment occurred at the end of Moses's 40-day encounter with God on the mountain, reinforcing the sacredness of the laws.

3. The Testimony "The tablets symbolized the covenant between God and Israel, serving as a testimony to their commitment to follow Him.

4. Foreshadowing Human Rebellion: "Despite this divine gift, in the following chapter *(Exodus 32)*, the Israelites fall into sin by worshiping the golden calf, leading Moses to break the tablets

in anger. This verse highlights God's direct involvement in guiding His people and serves as a reminder of the importance of obedience and covenant faithfulness.

The Lord will set forth justice on thy oppressors and deliver you out of the bondage of the gates and the clutches of the kingdom of darkness and its agents. So long you live in his righteousness and obedience.

The Finger of God in Creation and Provision

The finger of God is seen in his creation, as he formed the universe and provided for every need. His creative power is available to create provision, support and solutions in our lives.

Psalm 8:3 - "When I consider your heavens, the work of your fingers, the moon and the stars, which you have set in place."

The Finger of God in Writing Our Destiny

The finger of God is also seen in the way he writes our destinies. He has a plan and purpose for each of us, and his finger directs our steps according to his divine will.

Daniel 5:5 - "Suddenly the fingers of a human hand appeared and wrote on the plaster of the wall, near the lampstand in the royal palace. The king watched the hand as it wrote."

Memory Verse:

Your act of faith can activate God's intervention, and he will provide the instructions on what you should do and the way you should go. He will use anything and anyone to bless you, and often, he will pull you away from your comfort zone and move you to acquire and do new things. "Bring me a new bowl." *(2 Kings 2:20).*

The instructions of God will lead us out of bitter, barren places and starve out our problems, causing them to dry up from the root. In faith, you can speak and prophesy to any situation you encounter. You can use your faith to command a permanent solution.

Please understand when praying for God's intervention, the Lord God can give you revelations in dreams, visions, and through signs and wonders. He is not a man in which he would lie or a son of a man in which he would repent. The Lord can change his mind at any time. It doesn't mean that the revelation or the intended outcome has changed, but the instructions, directions, location, timing, and people may change. Do not allow this to discourage you or shake the foundation of your faith. When you are in uncertain conditions, you pray in faith, not in fear or out of desperation, but in knowing that all things work together for your greatest good.

The Finger of God in Creation and Provision

The finger of God is seen in His creation, as He formed the universe and provided for every need. His creative power is available to create provision, support, and solutions in our lives.

Psalm 8:3 – *"When I consider your heavens, the work of your fingers, the moon and the stars, which you have set in place."*

The Finger of God in Writing Our Destiny

The finger of God is also seen in the way He writes our destinies. He has a plan and purpose for each of us, and His finger directs our steps according to His divine will.

Daniel 5:5 – *"Suddenly the fingers of a human hand appeared and wrote on the plaster of the wall, near the lampstand in the royal palace. The king watched the hand as it wrote."*

Memory Verse:

Your act of faith can activate God's intervention, and He will provide instructions for what you should do and the way you should go. He will use anything and anyone to bless you. Often, He will pull you away from your comfort zone and move you to acquire and do new things. *"Bring me a new bowl"* (**2 Kings 2:20**).

The instructions of God will lead us out of bitter, barren places and starve out our problems, causing them to dry up from the root. In faith, you can speak and prophesy to any situation you encounter. You can use your faith to command a permanent solution.

Please understand: When praying for God's intervention, the Lord can give you revelations through dreams, visions, signs, and wonders. He is not a man, that He should lie, nor a son of man, that He should repent (**Numbers 23:19**). The Lord may change His methods—the instructions, directions, timing, or people involved—without altering His ultimate purpose. Do not let this discourage you or shake your faith. In uncertain times, pray in faith, not in fear or desperation, knowing that *all things work together for good* (**Romans 8:28**).

CHAPTER 12

Let us speak and pray.

These prayer points are inspired by Scriptures about the **"finger of God,"** which demonstrates His divine power, authority, and intervention. The finger of God represents His miraculous acts, His authority in creation, and His ability to bring change. Use these prayers to invoke God's power in your battles, relying on His authority for victory and deliverance.

1. **Father God,** whatsoever and whosoever You would use to locate me, make sure I am in the right place at the right time to receive Your divine instructions, in Jesus' mighty name.
2. **Finger of God,** arise and scatter the bitterness and barrenness from my land of promise, in the mighty name of Jesus Christ.
3. **Lord**, may Your mighty hand and outstretched arm intervene in every challenging situation in my life. Let Your finger bring an end to all afflictions and trials I face.
4. **Father,** let Your power be made manifest in my life. Show Your greatness through the works of Your hands in every area where I need deliverance.

5. In the name of Jesus, **Lord,** show me everything I need to know and tell me everything I need to hear to turn my life around for permanent solutions to my problems.
6. **O God**, arise and scatter by fire every doubt in my life that would uproot my faith, in Jesus' mighty name.
7. **Lord**, by Your finger, break every chain of oppression and deliver me from every form of captivity—whether spiritual, emotional, or physical.
8. **Father**, let Your kingdom come into my life. Let Your finger cast out every evil force working against me. Bring Your peace and freedom into my situation.
9. I command every power that has caused me to struggle now and in the past to be destroyed and burned to ashes, in Jesus' name.
10. **Every stronghold** in my life holding me down, release me now and burn to ashes!
11. **Lord**, let Your finger bring judgment against every enemy that rises against me. Vindicate me, and let justice prevail in every area where I have been wronged.
12. **Father**, establish Your righteousness in my life. Let Your finger writes Your laws on my heart and guide me to walk in Your truth and justice.
13. I decree and declare a **fresh and new anointing** over my water resources. I declare that they are not barren or bitter but sweet as honey!

14. **Holy Spirit**, heal me and restore my wasted years, in Jesus' mighty name.
15. **Finger of God**, touch and dispel every frustration I have ever carried, in the name of Jesus.
16. **Lord**, as You created the heavens and the earth with Your fingers, create new opportunities and solutions in my life. Provide for every need and open doors of blessing for me.
17. **Father**, let Your finger guide me in all my endeavors. Grant me wisdom and creativity to navigate every challenge and accomplish Your purpose for my life.
18. **Finger of God**, touch me and give me all-around peace in every situation, in the name of Jesus.
19. **Father God**, cleanse me of every tormenting, unclean, and dishonorable thing. Make me new and whole in Your holy light, in the name of Jesus.
20. **Every faulty, foul, unclean, and evil family foundation** I have inherited—O God of Elijah, arise and uproot it by fire, in the mighty name of Jesus!
21. **Every foundational and generational problem** from my father and mother that I have believed and carried—uproot it by force! Let it be destroyed and burned to ashes, in Jesus' name.
22. **Every internal and external battle** from evil family foundations causing delay and stagnation in my life—die by fire, in the name of Jesus!

23. I speak **life** into every miscarriage, dying, and bitter problem in my life, in the name of **Jesus**. *(Fixed spelling: "Jesue" → "Jesus")*
24. **Finger of God**, activate Your anointing fire in my life and make it permanent, in **Jesus' name**. *(Fixed spelling: "Jesue" → "Jesus")*
25. **Father God**, have mercy and deliver me from every secret torment that has plagued me, in Jesus' name. *(Fixed spelling: "secrete" → "secret")*
26. **O Lord**, anoint me with a heart of obedience and boldness to serve You unconditionally, in Jesus' name.
27. I declare and decree: **I am strong in the Lord and in the power of His might**, in the name of Jesus!
28. **Holy Spirit**, establish me for good works that will bring glory and testimony to Your name alone, in the name of Jesus.
29. **Lord**, let Your finger write my destiny according to Your will. Align my life with Your plans and purposes. Lead me to the path You have prepared for me.
30. **Father**, direct my steps with Your mighty hand. Let Your finger point the way I should go. Lead me into the fulfillment of Your promises by the blood of Jesus, in Jesus' mighty name.

Amen! Amen! Amen!!

Thank You, Father, for answered prayers!

CHAPTER 13

Faith Must Stand Trail

There are times when your faith must stand trial, and every part of your existence is tested and tried not because you are unworthy, but because you are the apple of God's eye, and He has invested His love and Spirit in thee for thee to prosper and live.

The Testing of Deliverance: A Trial of Faith

The concept of deliverance being tested is a profound and central theme in the Bible. It acknowledges that believers often face trials, challenges, and adversities in their journey of faith. These tests are not a reflection of unworthiness or divine rejection but rather an expression of God's love, refinement, and the deeper work He is doing in the life of the believer. The testing of faith is a process that leads to spiritual growth, refinement, and, ultimately, deliverance.

Let us explore how deliverance can be tested through trials, how these tests are not signs of rejection but of God's investment in us, and how the Bible presents examples of faith being tested.

1. Testing to Strengthen and Refine Faith

In the Bible, testing often serves to refine and purify a person's faith, drawing them closer to God and preparing them for greater things. This is sometimes referred to as *spiritual refinement* or *spiritual pruning*, where God shapes us into stronger, more dependent vessels.

Scriptural Example: James 1:2–4 *"Consider it pure joy, my brothers and sisters, whenever you face trials of many kinds because you know that the testing of your faith produces perseverance. Let perseverance finish its work so that you may be mature and complete, not lacking anything."*

- **Explanation:** James speaks directly to the believer's perspective during times of trial. While it may seem counterintuitive to find joy in hardship, these tests are the means through which our faith is refined. Trials produce perseverance, and perseverance matures our faith, making us complete. God's desire is not to harm us but to purify and strengthen us so that we lack nothing in our spiritual life.

In essence, the testing of your deliverance—when you face difficult circumstances—is not because you are unworthy but because God is preparing you to experience His fullness and to stand strong in faith.

Scriptural Example: 1 Peter 1:6–7 *"In all this, you greatly rejoice, though now, for a little while, you may have had to suffer grief in all kinds of trials. These have come so that the proven genuineness of your faith—of greater worth than gold,* *which perishes even though refined by fire may result in praise, glory, and honor when Jesus Christ is revealed."*

- **Explanation:** Peter compares the testing of faith to gold being refined by fire. Just as gold is purified by fire, our faith is purified through trials. The trials we face are not punishment but an opportunity to prove the genuineness and strength of our faith. When we endure trials, our faith becomes more precious than gold, leading to praise, glory, and honor when Christ returns.

2. Testing to Reveal and Develop God's Purpose

When God allows your deliverance to be tested, it is not merely a trial for the sake of suffering; it is part of His grand purpose for your life. God uses challenges to reveal His will, aligning you with His purposes and drawing you closer to Him.

Scriptural Example: Abraham's Test of Faith (Genesis 22:1–2, 9–12) *"Sometime later, God tested Abraham. He said to him, 'Abraham!' 'Here I am,' he replied. Then God said, 'Take your son, your only son, whom you love Isaac and go to the region of Moriah. Sacrifice him there as a burnt offering on a mountain I will show you.'"*

"When they reached the place God had told him about, Abraham built an altar there and arranged the wood on it. He bound his son Isaac and laid him on the altar, on top of the wood. Then he reached out his hand and took the knife to slay

his son. But the angel of the LORD called out to him from heaven, 'Abraham! Abraham!' 'Here I am,' he replied. 'Do not lay a hand on the boy,' he said. 'Do not do anything to him. Now I know that you fear God because you have not withheld from me your son, your only son.'" (Genesis 22:9–12, NIV)

- **Explanation:** Abraham's faith was tested when God asked him to sacrifice his beloved son, Isaac, the son promised to him by God. This test was meant not to harm Abraham or Isaac but to show Abraham's unwavering trust in God and to strengthen his commitment to God's promises. God's testing of Abraham reveals that His purpose was to establish Abraham as the father of faith, demonstrating the depth of his trust and submission to God's will.

The key point here is that sometimes God tests you in ways that appear difficult or beyond comprehension. However, such tests reveal your true devotion to God and position you to experience greater deliverance and blessings in the long run.

3. Testing to Prove God's Faithfulness

Tests are often allowed by God not just to refine your faith but to prove His own faithfulness. In difficult circumstances, when everything seems uncertain, God's deliverance proves that He is trustworthy and faithful to His promises.

Scriptural Example: The Israelites' Deliverance at the Red Sea (Exodus 14:10–14) *"As Pharaoh approached, the Israelites looked up, and there were the Egyptians, marching after them. They were terrified and cried out to the LORD. They said to Moses, 'Was it because there were no graves in Egypt that you brought us to the desert to die? What have you done to us by bringing us out of Egypt? Didn't we say to you in Egypt, "Leave us alone; let us serve the Egyptians"? It would have been better for us to serve the Egyptians than to die in the desert!' Moses answered the people, 'Do not be afraid. Stand firm, and you will see the deliverance the LORD will bring you today. The Egyptians you see today you will never see again. The LORD will fight for you; you need only to be still.'"*

- **Explanation:** As the Israelites were trapped between the Pharaoh's army and the Red Sea, they feared for their lives and questioned their deliverance. But Moses reassured them that God's power would deliver them, and God miraculously parted the Red Sea, allowing them to cross on dry land. The test of faith that the Israelites experienced was an opportunity for God to demonstrate His unmatched power and faithfulness.

This moment proved that deliverance comes not from human strength or strategy but from God's faithfulness. Sometimes, we may find ourselves in situations where our faith is tested to its limits, but God uses those moments to show that He alone is our deliverer.

4. Testing to Strengthen Our Character and Increase Our Spiritual Fruit

Tests also play a role in building the character of Christ in you and producing spiritual fruit. As you face trials, you develop qualities such as patience, perseverance, humility, and self-control.

Scriptural Example: Job's Testing (Job 1:6–12, Job 42:10–17) The story of Job is one of the clearest examples of a life being tested. Job was a righteous man who faced unimaginable suffering: he lost his wealth, his health, and his family. His faith was tested in the face of intense personal loss.

- **Explanation:** Job's testing was not a sign of divine displeasure but a test of the depth of his faith and a means to refine his character. Despite his suffering, Job never cursed God, and in the end, he was restored and blessed even more than before. God's faithfulness was revealed through Job's perseverance, and his story serves as a powerful example of how faith can be strengthened in the crucible of trials.

In Job's case, the trial was not about his worthiness but about God's glory being revealed through his perseverance. God allowed Job to endure great hardship, but through it, Job's character was strengthened, and his faith was purified.

When your deliverance is tested, it often happens because God has invested His love, His Spirit, and His promises in you. He desires for you to prosper—not just materially, but spiritually and emotionally—growing in His likeness.

- **God's love for you** means He doesn't leave you to your own devices but actively shapes you through trials to fulfill His purpose for your life.
- **The testing of faith** is a process that leads to greater maturity and completeness.
- **Deliverance** is often a testimony of God's faithfulness and power, showing you that He is with you through every trial and will deliver you according to His perfect will.

Ultimately, the Bible shows us that trials and testing are part of God's redemptive plan. They refine us, reveal God's purpose, prove His faithfulness, and build our character. Though the process may be challenging, it is always for the glory of God and the ultimate good of those who trust in Him.

Here are **7 key prayers** for deliverance and empowerment to overcome trials testing and stay motivated in your faith:

1. **Prayer for strength and endurance** – *Isaiah 40:31*
2. **Renewed mind and thoughts** – *Romans 12:2*
3. **Prayer for emotional stability and peace** – *Philippians 4:6–7*
4. **Prayer for divine guidance and direction** – *Proverbs 3:5–6*

5. **Prayer for faith to overcome doubt** – *Hebrews 11:1*
6. **Prayer for victory over temptation** – *1 Corinthians 10:13*
7. **Prayer for a heart of testimony and praise** – *Romans 8:28*

CHAPTER 14

No Fear Permitted

Fear is a powerful and subtle force that can act as a significant oppressor of faith, hindering spiritual growth, diminishing authority, and extinguishing the fire of belief. It often creeps into the hearts of believers, subtly or forcefully, undermining their trust in God's promises and power. Below are ways in which fear operates as an oppressor of faith and how it affects a believer's spiritual life:

1. Fear Undermines Trust in God's Promises

Faith is built on trust—trust that God will fulfill His promises, provide, and protect. Fear, however, shakes this trust. It causes doubt about God's ability or willingness to deliver on His Word. For instance, when faced with challenges such as illness, financial struggles, or relationship issues, fear can make a person question God's provision or His presence. The more a believer focuses on fear, the more they lose sight of God's faithfulness. Fear invites doubt, which erodes the foundation of faith.

- **Scriptural reference:** *"For God gave us a spirit not of fear but of power and love and self-control."* (2 Timothy 1:7). Fear here is contrasted with power, love, and a sound mind—essential elements for strong faith.

2. Fear Weakens Spiritual Resolve

Fear can paralyze believers, making them hesitant or unwilling to act in faith. For example, if someone is called to take a step of faith—such as forgiving someone, moving to a new place for ministry, or starting a new venture—they may become overwhelmed by the fear of failure, rejection, or the unknown. This fear keeps them from stepping into God's will and diminishes the strength of their spiritual resolve.

- **Scriptural reference:** *"Do not be afraid or discouraged, for the Lord your God will be with you wherever you go."* (Joshua 1:9). Fear can discourage believers from acting, but God's presence provides the courage needed.

3. Fear Creates Anxiety and Doubt

Fear often manifests as anxiety, worry, and dread, consuming the minds and hearts of believers. As worry takes root, it distracts them from God's promises and the spiritual peace that comes with trusting in Him. When anxiety takes hold, it clouds the mind, making it difficult to hear God's voice or perceive His guidance. This anxiety is a direct attack on the peace that accompanies faith.

- **Scriptural reference:** *"Do not be anxious about anything, but in everything, by prayer and petition, with thanksgiving, present your requests to God."* (Philippians 4:6). Anxiety is the opposite of peace, and through prayer, we are invited to release fear and embrace trust.

4. Fear Causes Spiritual Stagnation

Faith requires movement—whether stepping out in obedience, serving others, or trusting in God's provision. Fear, however, keeps believers stagnant. When fear takes over, it can lead to spiritual paralysis. Instead of growing in grace, experiencing God's power, or trusting Him in new ways, believers remain in their comfort zones, afraid to grow or change.

- **Scriptural reference:** *"So we have come to know and to believe the love that God has for us. God is love, and anyone who abides in love abides in God, and God abides in them."* (1 John 4:16). Fear prevents the believer from experiencing and abiding in God's love, which is essential for spiritual growth.

5. Fear Blocks Authority and Power

God has given believers authority in Christ to overcome the works of the enemy (Luke 10:19), walk in victory, and live out their purpose. Fear robs believers of this authority. When dominated by fear, they are unable to step into the power and dominion God has granted them. They may feel incapable or insufficient to confront challenges or engage in spiritual warfare because fear undermines their confidence in their identity in Christ.

- **Scriptural reference:** *"I can do all things through Christ who strengthens me."* (Philippians 4:13). Fear often makes believers feel weak, but Christ empowers them to face any challenge.

6. Fear Steals the Fire of Spiritual Passion

Spiritual fire is the passionate desire to seek God, worship Him, and live according to His will. Fear, however, extinguishes this fire. When believers are consumed by fear, it dampens their enthusiasm for spiritual pursuits. Instead of fervently seeking God's presence or boldly proclaiming the gospel, fear causes them to withdraw, retreat, and live in spiritual isolation. Fear replaces the fire of passion with a coldness of spirit.

- **Scriptural reference:** *"For the Spirit God gave us does not make us timid, but gives us power, love, and self-discipline."* (2 Timothy 1:7). The Holy Spirit empowers believers to live with passion and zeal, not with fear and timidity.

7. Fear Disconnects from the Source of Strength

Faith connects believers to God's strength, but fear disconnects them from that source. Just as faith enables believers to draw strength from God in times of weakness, fear leads them to rely on their own abilities or the world's solutions. When believers rely on their own understanding or resources, they lack the supernatural strength and wisdom God provides.

- **Scriptural reference:** *"The Lord is my light and my salvation—whom shall, I fear? The Lord is the stronghold of my life—of whom shall I be afraid?"* (Psalm 27:1). Fear causes believers to forget the source of their strength, which is God.

Declarations and Prayers of Unmovable, Unshakable, and Uncapturable Faith

1. **My Father, My Father, My Father**, I believe in Your power to restore and renew. Hear my cry; restore me and make me anew, in Jesus' mighty name.
2. **God of Jacob, Isaac, and Abraham**, strengthen my faith so I may trust You even in the most desolate situations, in the name of Jesus.
3. **God of Ezekiel**, help me to speak life, truth, and light over every dry place in every area of my life by the blood of Jesus.
4. **Father**, let Your finger point me in the right direction and lighten my darkness in all four directions, in the name of Jesus.
5. **O God, arise** and illuminate my pathway; give me clarity in every decision concerning my life, in Jesus' mighty name.
6. **Almighty God**, stretch forth Your arm of power and fight for me against every unseen obstacle blocking my destiny in the mighty name of Jesus.
7. **Man of War**, break every chain, remove every obstacle, and deliver me from every challenge standing in my way, in Jesus' mighty name.

8. **Lord**, breathe Your breath of life on me. **Holy Spirit**, fill me with Your life-giving power, in Jesus' mighty name.

9. **O Breath of the Great I AM**, revive my faith, revive my spirit, renew my strength by fire, and restore my joy, in Jesus' mighty name.

10. **God of Daniel**, fill me with Your spirit of wisdom, understanding, and knowledge. Teach me to be steadfast and unmovable in my faith, in Jesus' mighty name.

11. **I denounce and reject** all negative, false thoughts and statements that rob me of faith in God's promises for my life in the name of Jesus. *(Say this 21 times.)*

12. **The God who answers prayers**, answer my prayers by fire, in Jesus' mighty name.

13. **I reject** every negative thought that dilutes my faith in the Word of God, in the mighty name of Jesus.

14. **God of Meshach, Shadrach, and Abednego**, fill me with fire-burning faith that outlasts and surpasses threats in the face of danger, in Jesus' mighty name.

15. **Lord**, teach me to obey Your voice like Ezekiel, in the name of Jesus.

16. **Lord**, help me to trust in Your Word and act in faith, knowing that You are faithful and will fulfill all Your promises.

17. **God of restoration**, I ask You to renew the broken areas of my life.

18. **God of love and light**, heal my heart, restore my relationships, and breathe new life and power into my purpose, in Jesus' holy name.
19. **Lord**, I declare victory over every seen and unseen obstacle in my life by the power in the blood of Jesus.
20. **By Your power and authority, Lord**, I will walk forward in confidence, knowing that nothing is impossible for You for those who believe in the powerful name of Jesus Christ.

CHAPTER 15

What Faith Can Do that No Man Can Not Do

Let us declare with boldness the power of faith and all that it can accomplish. Faith is able to outshine, outmaneuver, and disrupt every plan of backwardness and failure the enemy has set against your life. You are more than a conqueror; you are a warrior, and you are the apple of God's eye. No weapon formed against you shall prosper (Isaiah 54:17). Your faith is the key to your success—both internally and externally—as you rise and shine. The time for your breakthrough is now, and nothing can stand in the way of what God has destined for you. Your time has come, and your faith will carry you forward into the victory that is already yours.

Let us speak and declare what Faith in God Can Do:

1. Faith can open doors of opportunity and progress.
2. Faith can refurbish forgotten ideas and plans.
3. Faith can build a ladder of promotion and elevation in my destiny.
4. Faith can open doors that no man can open and close doors that no man can close (Revelation 3:7).

5. Faith can release heavenly-stored blessings from my storehouse into my hands.
6. Faith can take me where no man or woman can stop me.
7. Faith can deliver me out of every negative stronghold of failure.
8. Faith can restore the years the locusts and caterpillars have eaten (Joel 2:25).
9. Faith can heal and restore strength to my bones.
10. Faith can arrest every limitation in my life right now.
11. Faith can take me from the back of the line to the front of the line.
12. Faith can make me an overnight success.
13. Faith without works is dead (James 2:26).
14. Faith will make a mountain for my enemies and a river for my success.
15. Faith will make the resources of my water sweet.
16. Faith can strengthen my shield of protection (Shekinah crown of glory).
17. Faith can make my enemies my footstool (Psalm 110:1).
18. Faith will make the evil plans of my enemies fail foolishly.
19. Faith can give the breath of God's nostrils to anything dead or dying in my life.
20. Faith can open endless doors of blessings and favor in every department of my life.
21. Faith can deliver me from the traps of the enemy.

22. Faith can make my enemies foolish.
23. Faith can kill every Goliath and hang every Haman in my life.
24. Faith will trouble my troublers and destroy my destroyers in any area of my life.
25. Faith can give me the blinding light of protection in every situation of darkness.
26. Faith can dispel confusion and anxiety.
27. Faith can remove the cataracts from my spiritual eyes.
28. Faith can open the eyes of the heart and remove the stones of limitations.
29. Faith can break every prison door of captivity and dormancy in my life.
30. Faith can open the door to receive answers and resolve any problem that the curiosity of man cannot locate.
31. Faith can make a path in the valley and a river in the desert (Isaiah 43:19).
32. Faith can arrest and locate my destiny helpers.
33. Faith can destroy sickness and disease in my body.
34. Faith can put my naysayers to shame and reproach.
35. Faith can destroy every invisible embargo to success in every department of my life.
36. Faith can destroy the enemy of my progress and arrest the arrows of fear.
37. Faith can open doors to opportunities that my skills alone cannot access.

38. Faith can seat me in high places.
39. Faith can supply all my needs and release resources to me that have been previously held by demonic forces in the second heaven.
40. Faith can make God my refuge and strength, a very present help in trouble (Psalm 46:1).
41. Faith as small as a mustard seed can move any mountain (Matthew 17:20), outwit any challenger, and resolve every problem present in my life.
42. My faith shall prevail in every department of my life, and I shall rise and shine.
43. In the Scriptures, it is written: *"The just shall live by faith"* (Hebrews 10:38). I make a conscious decision to live and walk by faith in the name of Jesus.
44. Lord Jesus, it is written: *"Faith comes by hearing"* (Romans 10:17). Close my ears to everything the enemy of my progress can use to build fear in my heart, in the name of Jesus.
45. Faith can move mountains spiritually and physically.
46. Faith can heal the sick and raise the dead.
47. Faith can provide divine provisions in times of need where no man can provide.
48. Faith can redirect my destiny by breaking every chain of adversity and bondage.
49. Faith can catapult you to achieve the impossible beyond human understanding and ability.

50. Faith can bring calm in the middle of the most challenging situations.
51. Faith can provide divine protection that no human security system can guarantee.
52. Faith can deliver my destiny and life out of bondage.
53. Faith can break yokes and various forms of bondage and captivity.
54. Faith can call forth things that are not as though they were (Romans 4:17).
55. My declarations have become my possession, and I shall have what I have declared today.

CHAPTER 16

Activation of Great Faith

Four Examples of Great Faith in Scripture

1. The Faith of the Soldier: The Centurion *(Matthew 8:5–13; Luke 7:1–10)*

Story: A Roman centurion approached Jesus, asking Him to heal his servant. He expressed unshakable faith by saying Jesus did not need to come to his house—only speak the word, and his servant would be healed.

- **Faith:** The centurion recognized Jesus' authority and trusted His power without requiring physical proof.
- **Jesus' Response:** Jesus marveled, saying, *"I have not found such great faith, not even in Israel."*

2. The Faith of the Widow: The Widow of Zarephath *(1 Kings 17:8–16)*

Story: During a severe drought, God sent Elijah to a widow in Zarephath. Despite having only a handful of flour and oil, she obeyed Elijah's request to feed him first, trusting God's promise to provide.

- **Faith:** She surrendered her last provisions, relying on God's word through Elijah.

- **Outcome:** Her faith was rewarded—the flour and oil lasted throughout the famine.

3. The Faith of a mother: The Canaanite Woman *(Matthew 15:21–28)*

Story: A Canaanite woman begged Jesus to heal her demon-possessed daughter. Though Jesus initially tested her, she persisted, humbly accepting His analogy of "dogs" eating crumbs.

- **Faith:** She demonstrated unwavering trust in Jesus' power and mercy despite cultural barriers.
- **Jesus' Response:** He commended her *"great faith"* and healed her daughter.

4. The Faith of a Father: Jairus *(Mark 5:21–24, 35–43; Luke 8:40–56)*

Story: Jairus, a synagogue leader, pleaded with Jesus to heal his dying daughter. Even when told she had died, he clung to hope.

- **Faith:** Jairus believed Jesus could restore his daughter—even from death.
- **Outcome:** Jesus raised her to life, affirming Jairus' faith.

CHAPTER 17

Prayer of Praise and Thanksgiving:

Heavenly Father,

I thank You for revealing the incredible power of faith and how it transforms the course of my life by providing solutions to every challenge I face. Thank You for Your mighty hand of protection, keeping me safe and out of the enemy's reach. I am grateful for Your tender mercies and the boundless grace You continually pour over my life and destiny.

Lord, I praise You for being the Way maker in every area of my life and for commanding Your angels to watch over me. Thank You for Your miracle-working power that dispels all darkness and pushes back the forces of evil. You are awesome, Father! You have moved mountains on my behalf and shielded me from the storms of failure and defeat.

As I rise like an eagle, soaring with renewed strength and boldness in Your Word, I decree and declare Your salvation over my life. I trust that You, Lord, are my stronghold—my Alpha and Omega, the Author and Finisher of my faith. I stand firm in the belief that all I have prayed for today shall come to pass.

Thank You, Lord, for answered prayers. It is established, and it is done, in Jesus' name. **Amen.**

CHAPTER 18

My Time to Rise: Tested Faith

Now that we understand that faith comes from hearing and recognizing the many powerful things it can do let us also consider the times when our faith is tested. Action is required to move things forward, and along the way, you will encounter obstacles that challenge your standing. In these moments, you must refuse to entertain fear in any form. Whatever must be done to move forward, do it with courage. Remember, patience is the tool that exposes deception. During times of testing, your faith is called to stand strong, endure the trial, and emerge refined.

Expect resistance to your rising and especially to your shining. You may be surprised by those who, secretly in their hearts, wish for your failure and shame. But as you walk confidently toward your destiny, rising and shining, remember you are not alone. The Lord is your strength, and He is with you every step of the way. The Blood of Jesus is the most powerful defense in existence, protecting you against every attack and against the schemes of the enemy. Your success is guaranteed through your acts of faith and obedience. Every step you take is ordered by the Lord and cannot be manipulated, bewitched, captured, or stopped.

Throughout Scripture, we see multiple examples of resistance and opposition during the process of rebuilding and renewing a covenant with the Lord. These challenges can manifest in many forms: problems, situations, projects, relationships, or even financial shortages or excesses. In these times of testing, we must remain vigilant and recognize when we need to shift our posture—both in our thinking and in our vision. Change is constant, and it is a necessary part of growth, both internally and externally.

The first step you must take is to thank the Lord that you are worthy of the signs and wonders He is working in your life. These challenges are not only a testament to your faith but also a reflection of God's glory and His faithfulness in your journey.

In **Judges 5:6–7**, Deborah declared, *"The highways were deserted, and the travelers walked along the byways; village life ceased, it ceased in Israel, until I, Deborah, arose, arose a mother in Israel."* This passage is a powerful reminder to stay encouraged during every phase of your rebuilding and rising process.

As we navigate this phase of rebuilding and rebranding our lives, it is crucial to remain watchful for the opportunities available to us. Often, we approach these opportunities with a narrow, closed-minded perspective—believing that we know exactly how things should unfold or who should help us on our journey. My friends, I urge you to recognize that such thinking can be dangerous to your progress. It limits what God and faith can accomplish together.

When we become attached to our own way of thinking or to a fixed idea of how things should be, we risk impairing our connection to our destiny and hindering our ability to hear God's guidance. This mindset can stagnate, strangle, and delay not only your own rising but also the rising of others because we do not operate in isolation in the body of Christ.

In **1 Corinthians 10:23**, Paul reminds us, *"'I have the right to do anything,' you say—but not everything is beneficial. 'I have the right to do anything'—but not everything is constructive."* While we have the freedom to make choices, it's crucial to remember that not every decision leads to growth or contributes to building up the body of Christ. Our freedom must be guided by wisdom and discernment. Let us strive to remain open, thoughtful, and fully aligned with God's perfect plan for our lives, recognizing that not every option, though permissible, is beneficial for our spiritual journey or the advancement of His Kingdom.

The 7 Issues and Opposition to Your Rising and Rebuilding

"When Sanballat the Horonite and Tobiah the Ammonite official heard about this, they were very much disturbed that someone had come to promote the welfare of the Israelites."

But when Sanballat the Horonite, Tobiah the Ammonite official, and Geshem the Arab heard about it, they mocked and ridiculed us. "What is this you are doing?" they asked. "Are you rebelling against the king?" (**Nehemiah 2:10, 2:19**)

In this Scripture, you will note that seven themes of opposition experienced by Nehemiah on his divine assignment can be applied to various situations in our own lives. Please read each theme described below and refer to the Scripture above:

1. **External Opposition:** When the Lord is initiating a positive change in your life, there will be sources threatened by the changes. There will always be external forces human personalities, regions, territories, or systems, both physically and spiritually that are deeply disturbed by the work God has called you to do. They will resist progress, growth, or rebuilding because it disrupts their agenda. Sanballat and Tobiah represented figures of influence who were disturbed by Nehemiah's concern for the well-being of Jerusalem. Additionally, when the Lord God calls someone to rise and rebuild, opposition can arise from both visible and invisible personalities who are afraid of losing power and control.
2. **Criticism and Mockery:** Your adversaries will mock and criticize you as you take the courage to walk in your divine destiny's calling. This can manifest in the form of people, unexpected situations, obligations, or sickness being used to

delay and derail your efforts. The opposition can come from those you love and respect, and their job in that moment is to sow seeds of discouragement. They do this through words of contempt and doubt so that you will forget or abandon God's assignment. Criticism and mockery are common tools of opposition. When Nehemiah began his work, his opponents belittled his and the Lord's efforts by accusing Nehemiah of rebellion (witchcraft). As you are called to step out in faith, you must not be dismayed by the ridicule and accusations that aim to discourage you or make the task ahead seem impossible or foolish.

3. **Questioning Intentions:** Opposition may come in the form of questioning your motives, accusations of wrongdoing, and misrepresentation of your intentions. Depending on your upbringing and/or experiences, this may discourage or disappoint you. Who does not want the support of the people they care about or respect? You must never forget: when you are building something for God, people may challenge the legitimacy of your calling and authority in that area, subject, or importance.

4. **Doubt and Intimidation:** The enemies of Nehemiah were not just displeased with his assignment, but they actively tried to create fear by questioning his motives, suggesting his actions were rebellious and dangerous. Intimidation can make you magnify your own insecurities and make you second-guess the

instructions of the Lord God's purpose. Those who are grieved by your progress and your calling want first to discourage you. They create doubt to make you believe the task to which you are called is too great for you, too impossible for you. The doubt can cause you to stumble and fall by weakening your faith and resolve. Remember: with God, all things are possible!

5. **Hidden Agendas, Political Pressures, and False Allegations:** Whenever you receive an assignment or task from the Lord, He has already calculated your needs and has staked out the opposition. He will put measures in place without the knowledge of your enemies. This is why it is important to guard your garment of glory and faith with perfect anger. You see, Sanballat, Tobiah, and Geshem accused Nehemiah of attempting to rebel against the king. The truth is that Nehemiah had the king's support, but they tried to paint him as a traitor. Similarly, those answering the Lord God's call can and will often face false accusations or political pressures. This tactic is designed to undermine the credibility, legality, authority, and ability of the believer.

6. **Internal Resistance and Discouragement (Implied):** The possibility of failure can be an internal factor of influence, and the worry of being on the receiving end of the enemy's retaliation for such boldness and courageousness is a recipe for discouragement. Doubt, weariness, and the negative influences of others can keep you from completing your God-given

assignment. Often, I have heard people say, *"Everything I try to do, someone opposes me, or something bad always happens. I don't have the resources; I am not smart enough, or that's too difficult for me to do."* Know this, beloved: your prayer request must include a request for a stronger backbone and faith to stand and put on the full armor of God in accordance with **Ephesians 6:12–18**.

7. **Testing of Leadership and Conviction: (Nehemiah 2:18)** *"And I told them of the hand of my God which had been good upon me and of the king's words that he had spoken to me. So, they said, 'Let us rise up and build.' Then they set their hands to this good work."* Nehemiah's leadership was tested through opposition. Remember that opposition may come in the way of lack of support, finances, or resources needed to complete the task. Nehemiah had to convince the people that God's hand was with him and that the task was not only possible but divinely ordained. When God calls you to lead a work of restoration, your faith, vision, and ability to inspire will be tested and tried by the opposition.

You do not know the hearts of men. You may lack the discernment to recognize demonic agents of progress. There are people you know and trust as well as strangers who will hear of your God-given plans and rage against your assignment. Unbeknownst to them, your steps have been **ordered, protected, and fortified by the King of Kings and**

Lord of Lords (Psalm 37:23). Beloved, you will be shocked by the faces of your "enemies of progress," even those in your own household, assigned to **kill, steal, and destroy** (John 10:10) your divine destiny. Remember Adam and Eve and Samson: their downfall came when an external enemy used a trusted insider to dismantle God's ordained plans.

How to Flex Spiritual Authority and Faith

Nehemiah's response to opposition is our model. He stood resolute, trusting God's plan and power. His faith in divine favor overcame every challenge. This passage reminds us that **when God calls you to rebuild or restore, opposition is inevitable, but His purpose will prevail** if we trust Him and stay focused.

1. **Recognize God's Calling:** Like Nehemiah, acknowledge you are called by God. Trust that **He will provide for what He commands** (Philippians 4:19).
2. **Pray for Wisdom:** Nehemiah prayed before acting (Nehemiah 1:4). Seek God's guidance in every decision, especially under opposition.
3. **Declare God's Authority:** Nehemiah proclaimed, *"The God of heaven Himself will prosper us"* (Nehemiah 2:20). Speak this over your obstacles.

4. **Stay Focused:** Nehemiah ignored mockery and threats (Nehemiah 6:3). Fix your eyes on the mission; let God handle distractions.
5. **Guard Your Mind:** When doubt arises, remember: *"Greater is He who is in you than he who is in the world"* (1 John 4:4).

Be protective of your plans. Your personal relationship with God grants unique insight not everyone will understand. Your goals may seem impossible to those with limited vision. Do not let their doubt infect your faith. **You are not a recycling bin for others' fear.** This is your time to **rise and shine** (Isaiah 60:1) today!

The Confidence and Faith to Rebuild

"'I also told them of the hand of my God, which had been good upon me, and also of the king's words that he had spoken to me. So they said, "Let us rise up and build." Then they set their hands to this good work.' (Nehemiah 2:18 NKJV)."

This proves God's goodness, paired with faith, moves mountains. Speak with boldness, no matter your past struggles. Lift your hands to the Almighty and declare your need for His **fire and power** to ignite your aspirations. Let faith—not fear—fuel your destiny. As you speak your vision, you summon its manifestation in the spiritual realm (Mark 11:23).

God's Guarantee to Prosper You

"'Then I replied to them, "The God of heaven will make us prosper, and we His servants will arise and build, but you have no portion or right or claim in Jerusalem."' (Nehemiah 2:20)."

This echoes His promise: *"For I know the plans I have for you,"* declares the Lord, *"plans to prosper you and not to harm you, plans to give you hope and a future."'* (Jeremiah 29:11). When faith wavers, remember: **His plans are irrevocable** (Romans 11:29).

This does not mean setbacks won't come. Your timing may differ from God's. Paths may detour; allies may change; resources may arrive unexpectedly. These are the trials of rising in divine alignment.

Divine Appointment of Support

"'Then I said to the king, "If it pleases the king, let letters be given to me for the governors of the region beyond the river, that they must permit me to pass through till I come to Judah, and a letter to Asaph the keeper of the king's forest, that he must give me timber to make beams for the gates of the citadel… and for the house that I will occupy." And the king granted them to me according to the good hand of my God upon me.' (Nehemiah 2:7-8 NKJV)."

Support for your dreams may come through mentors, books, sermons, or divine connections. Define support biblically **God often sends**

help in unexpected ways (Isaiah 43:19). Stay grounded in His Word to steward it well.

Prayer Letter of provisional needs. (Inspired by Nehemiah's favor before the king – Nehemiah 2:4-8)

1. Father, just as You granted Nehemiah favor before the king, let Your favor go before me. Open doors of provision and make a way where there is no way. In Jesus' name, Amen. (Proverbs 3:4)

2. O Lord, you are Jehovah Jireh, my Provider. Release every resource needed to accomplish the vision You have given me. Let nothing be lacking. In Jesus' name, Amen. (Philippians 4:19)

3. I command every spirit of delay, lack, and financial hindrance assigned against my destiny to be destroyed by the fire of God! I call forth abundance and overflow. In Jesus' name, Amen. (Deuteronomy 8:18)

4. Father, send me the right people—destiny helpers, investors, and supporters—who will stand with me to fulfill Your ordained plans. Let divine connections be established. In Jesus' name, Amen. (Isaiah 60:10)

5. O Lord, let the gates of provision be opened for me. Grant me access to platforms, partnerships, and places of influence that align with Your purpose for my life. In Jesus' name, Amen. (Revelation 3:8)

6. Every Sanballat and Tobiah spirit assigned to hinder my work, be silenced! I rebuke every distraction and opposition. I will build, restore, and accomplish God's vision for my life. In Jesus' name, Amen. (Nehemiah 6:9)
7. Father, let there be a supernatural acceleration of provision and breakthroughs. What should take years, let it manifest speedily by Your power. In Jesus' name, Amen. (Amos 9:13)
8. O Lord, as You provide, give me wisdom to manage resources well. Let me be a faithful steward, using everything for Your glory. In Jesus' name, Amen. (James 1:5)
9. I decree and declare that every financial provision and resource I receive is covered under the blood of Jesus. No devourer, thief, or loss shall come near my storehouse. In Jesus' name, Amen. (Malachi 3:11)
10. Father, as Nehemiah boldly asked the king for what he needed, give me the courage to step out in faith and make bold moves for the vision You have placed in my heart. In Jesus' mighty name, Amen. (2 Timothy 1:7)
11. Lord, order my steps and give me a divine strategy to build, expand, and establish what You have called me to do. Show me the right people, places, and timing. In Jesus' mighty name, Amen. (Proverbs 16:9)
12. Father, I thank You in advance for provision, breakthroughs, and answered prayers. I decree that it is done, and I will testify

of Your faithfulness. In Jesus' name, Amen! (1 Thessalonians 5:18)

Destiny of Unsolicited Divine Assistance: So, the king said, "Why do you look so sad? You're not sick. Something must be bothering you." Even though I was frightened, I answered, "Your Majesty, I hope you live forever! I feel sad because the city where my ancestors are buried is in ruins, and its gates have been burned down." (Nehemiah 2:2)

The above text shows the favor of the Lord on Nehemiah's heart's desires. *Where does my help come from? My help comes from the LORD, the Maker of heaven and earth.* You see, the Lord will send unsolicited divine assistance when He is the Author and Finisher of your plans and steps.

The destiny of unsolicited divine assistance shows up multiple times in the Bible. Each hero had a destiny that was fulfilled through the divine assistance and planning of the Lord. They were able to overcome obstacles of any severity through His will and divine help. For example:

- When David's father sent him on an errand to his brothers, he defeated Goliath.
- Rahab assisted two spies sent by Joshua to gather intelligence about Jericho before its conquest. Jehu was anointed and inducted as a king to destroy Jezebel.

- Paul's nephew provided intel that intercepted the plans to kill Paul.
- Ruth stayed with Naomi after the death of her husband and later married Boaz.
- David sought to bless the remaining members of Saul's household by providing them a place at his royal table. The blind man was carried to the fountain after lying lame for 38 years.

The list goes on and on. I could spend hours recounting the times the Lord has sent me unsolicited help—divine interventions I didn't ask for but desperately needed. *The joy of the Lord is our strength and our present help in times of trouble.* Let us act and stand up as we begin to pray now on the revelation wonders of our rising in this season.

Prayer Points:

1. **May every** envious evil force gathered for my failure **be** exposed and disgraced in the name of Jesus.
2. **Every** hidden pattern actively seeks my downfall (**let them take my place**). **May they** be exposed and disgraced in the name of Jesus.
3. I command every power boasting that I will not rise, build, and succeed: **"Be silenced and burn to ashes!"** in the name of Jesus.
4. Every evil conspiracy gathered, praying for my downfall and failure **you are liars! Backfire by fire and burn to ashes!**

5. **May every** spiritual and physical evil eye of jealousy and envy plotting against my plans and dreams **to slow me down be scattered by fire** in the name of Jesus.
6. **Against** any envious power, praying against my destiny helpers, **O God, arise!** Put them to shame and turn their prayers to foolishness.
7. Every embargo and blockage against me and my divine destiny helpers **be destroyed by fire, by force!**
8. Every distraction raised against me to impede my progress, **I terminate and roast you by fire** in the name of Jesus.
9. No matter how difficult my life has been, **I receive the power, authority, and fresh fire to pursue and rebuild** my life, business, ministry, and wealth in Jesus' name.
10. Oh Lord, if You do not help me, I will fail. Father, release Your anointing of fire upon me **now** so that I may succeed in Jesus' mighty name.
11. Father, release all the messages of Your Word that I need to hear **to pursue and charge forward**. Send them now in the name of Jesus Christ.
12. Strange enemies, strange problems, strange battles against my destiny helpers—**die by fire and die by thunder** in the name of Jesus.
13. O Lord, release quality men and women to help me in my restoration and rising in Jesus' name.

14. Father God, release upon me **provisional help** to assist me with my goals, covered by the blood of Jesus, in Jesus' holy name.
15. O Lord, open the book of remembrance and grace to remember me for Your good in the name of Jesus.
16. **May the** mercy of the Most High God make a way for me—**make a path in the valley and a river in the desert**—by the blood of Jesus, in the name of Jesus.
17. I shall arise and shine in every department of my life in the name of Jesus.
18. Powers assigned to attack me with problems without solutions—**you are liars! Catch fire and burn to ashes!**
19. Holy Spirit, set me apart by Your favor and grace **through** the blood of Jesus, in Jesus' name.
20. I receive the **provisional keys of David** to the goodness kept in God's Heavenly Bank for me in the name of Jesus.
21. O Lord, sweeten the story of my testimony with **the milk and honey of heaven** in the mighty name of Jesus.

Yoke Breaking Confession Prayer

Dear Heavenly Father,

I come before You in the mighty name of the resurrected Jesus, whom I serve and to whom I belong. I stand in the authority of Your Word, determined to enforce Your divine will and purpose while pushing back the schemes of darkness—both seen and unseen.

I decree and declare that no weapon formed against me—whether emotional, financial, social, physical, psychological, interpersonal, spiritual, or organizational—shall prosper. I affirm that my weapons of warfare are not carnal but mighty through You, O God. I pull down every stronghold, cast down vain imaginations, and bring every thought captive to the obedience of Christ.

By the anointing of the Lord God of Elijah, I destroy every yoke, chain, rod, silver cord, ley line, and threefold cord designed to hinder or oppress me. I declare that my soul, spirit, mind, and every organ in my body align with Your divine order and protocol. I proclaim healing and wholeness over my life, for sickness, disease, and death have no authority over me.

I establish divine boundaries and parameters, legislating the principles of Your Kingdom to govern every area of my life. I overturn every diabolical judgment, mandate, and decree that opposes Your will for my family, health, finances, ministry, business, and career. I nullify and overrule every negative word or decision spoken against me and those I love.

I take control over the realms of the earth and the heavens—the airways, galaxies, systems, elements, environments, and every sphere of influence—declaring Your sovereign rule. With Your strength, Lord, I declare that I can run through troops and leap over walls. You are the God of Abraham, Isaac, and Jacob, who equips me with power, makes my way perfect, and teaches my hands to war and my fingers to fight.

You are my Rock, my Shield, my Strong Tower, and my ever-present help in trouble. I dedicate myself to honoring and following You all the days of my life.

In the mighty and matchless name of Jesus, I pray. Amen.

My Time Has Come Rise and Shine

We have discussed throughout the book how important faith is and how it can transform your life. You have announced through your boldness the declaration of what faith can do and how to apply it in every area of your life. In this section, you are standing tall, head held high, back straight, and marching forward in the light of the Almighty by your faith as you believe your time has come.

Memory Verse:

"Arise, shine, for your light has come! And the glory of the Lord is risen upon you. For behold, the darkness shall cover the earth, and deep darkness the people; but the Lord will arise over you, and His glory will be seen upon you. The Gentiles shall come to your light, and kings to the brightness of your rising." **(Isaiah 60:1-3)**. The most important part is to **arise**—meaning to raise up, get up, and walk upright in the eyes of the Lord. Our Father has redeemed you, and we shall rise and not fall, for this is the inheritance and destiny of the children of the Lord. It must be a priority to live in the promise of the Living God. If we are not living out the promises made to each one of us, we must re-evaluate our lives and assess where we are lacking the power and glory of the fruit of the Spirit.

It is not natural for the children of God to lack or fail to possess the power, anointing, yoke-breaking fire, and thunderous lightning power from the glory of God. If you are not a carrier of God's fire, I encourage you to quickly find a true deliverance ministry of God that can plead for the mercy and grace of God to cleanse your life with the blood of Jesus. *For we walk by faith and not by sight* **(2 Corinthians 5:7)**. You see, you can't rise and shine if you are not living by faith. Faith removes obstacles, gives life to the dead, and calls forth things that do not yet exist in the physical as though they did **(Romans 4:17-18)**.

"So shall My word be that goes forth from My mouth; it shall not return to Me void, but it shall accomplish what I please, and it shall prosper in the thing for which I sent it." **(Isaiah 55:11)**

"For by grace you have been saved through faith, and that not of yourselves; it is the gift of God, not of works, lest anyone should boast. For we are His workmanship, created in Christ Jesus for good works, which God prepared beforehand that we should walk in them." **(Ephesians 2:8-10)**

The Power of the Spoken Word of Faith:

We know the very foundation of this world was built by the words of God because *in the beginning was the Word, and the Word was with God, and the Word was God* (John 1:1).

The story of Ezekiel and the valley of dry bones, found in **Ezekiel 37:1–14**, is a profound illustration of God's power to restore life, hope, and purpose to seemingly hopeless situations. In the vision, God leads Ezekiel to a valley filled with dry bones and commands him to prophesy to them. As Ezekiel obeys, the bones come together, are covered with flesh, and finally, receive the breath of life. This miraculous event symbolizes God's ability to revive and restore not only individuals but also nations, no matter how desolates their circumstances.

Understanding Ezekiel's Prophecy

1. **The Valley of Dry Bones**: This represents situations of hopelessness, defeat, or spiritual death in our lives. Like the dry bones, we may feel lifeless and disconnected, but God sees potential and purpose even in our most barren seasons.
2. **The Finger of God**: God's power and authority bring restoration. Just as the finger of God wrote the Ten Commandments and performed miracles in Egypt, His intervention is precise and purposeful. When He moves, transformation occurs.
3. **The Arm of God**: The arm of God symbolizes strength and might. It is by His mighty arm that He redeems, rescues, and delivers. With God's arm working in our lives, no obstacle is too great to overcome.
4. **Faith and Obedience**: Ezekiel's faith and obedience to speak life into the dry bones demonstrate the power of aligning with God's will. Our faith activates God's promises, and our personal prophecy—speaking His Word over our lives—brings His plans into reality.

5. **The Breath of Life**: God's Spirit brings vitality and renewal. The breath entering the bones represents the Holy Spirit, who empowers us to rise above challenges and live abundantly.

Moving Forward with Faith and Prophecy

When we face obstacles or seasons of despair, we can lean on the power of God's Word, light, and Spirit. Speaking life, declaring His promises, and trusting in His power helps us move forward with courage and purpose. God's finger points to the details; His arm fights for us, and our faith bridges His promises with our reality. *In the beginning, God created the heavens and the earth*, and He said, *Let there be light*. The light of God shines before you as you speak in faith and the power of God's promises for your life.

Oh God, Arise Declarations of Faith & Power
FAITH DECLARATIONS TO IGNITE YOUR SPIRIT

(Speak these with fire, authority, and unshakable confidence!)

1. **God, arise in my life today**, and let Your power break every chain of limitation, releasing me into the fullness of my destiny! *(Isaiah 60:1)*
2. **God, arise and renew my strength** so that I may soar like an eagle and overcome every obstacle standing before me! *(Isaiah 40:31)*
3. **God, arise and fill me** with wisdom, clarity, and boldness so I walk confidently in the path You've set before me! *(Proverbs 3:5-6)*
4. **God, arise and ignite my heart with hope**—for with You, *all things are possible*, and nothing can hinder my success! *(Matthew 19:26)*
5. **God, arise and shift my perspective**! Let me see *opportunities* in every challenge and stride boldly in Your divine purpose. *(Romans 8:28)*
6. **God, arise and silence every voice** of doubt, fear, and discouragement! You are my strength—**I will not be moved!** *(Psalm 16:8)*

7. **God, arise and pour out Your favor** upon me! Bless my efforts, and let my work bear fruit for Your glory. *(Psalm 90:17)*
8. **God, arise and heal every wound within me**. Restore my soul with Your peace and lead me into victory! *(Psalm 147:3)*
9. **God, arise and strengthen my faith**! With You, I'll move mountains, speak life, and declare Your greatness! *(Mark 11:23)*
10. **God, arise and be glorified** in my life, work, and relationships! Let Your Kingdom come, and You will be done in me. *(Matthew 6:10)*
11. **Oh God, arise and dispel** every spiritual weakness and lukewarmness in my life! *(Revelation 3:16)*
12. **Oh God, arise and show me mercy**—for now is my time to **rise and shine**; my season has come! *(Isaiah 60:1, Ecclesiastes 3:1)*

I shall raise for my time is now

Prayer Points

1. Thank You, Lord, for the breath and the gift of life in the name of Jesus.
2. Thank You, Lord, for the salvation of my soul and for counting me worthy.
3. Lord, identify and anoint me with Your oil of fire so that I stand out and am recognized as one of Your very own, in the name of Jesus.
4. Thank You, Father, for Your divine hedge of protection and for being a stronghold over my life and destiny in the name of Jesus.
5. Lord Jesus, let Your will become a strong tower and cornerstone in every department of my life, soaked by the blood of Jesus, in Jesus' mighty name.
6. O Lord, arise and anoint my life with fresh oil and fire for a turn-around bumper harvest this year, in the name of Jesus.
7. I shall arise and shine, for my light has come, in the mighty name of Jesus Christ.
8. O head of mine, I command you to arise and shine right now, for my time has come—that the glory of the Lord shall distinguish me, in the name of Jesus.
9. O God, arise and make me a carrier of Your power, fire, grace, favor, and glory in the name of Jesus.

10. Lord, let Your glory set me apart and shine brightly upon my life in the name of Jesus.

11. I come against, trample down, and put under my feet every power trying to quench my holy fire and squash my shine in the mighty name of Jesus Christ.

12. Lord, raise Your holy anger against every satanic agent of darkness identifying my rise and shine for failure. You are a liar! Backfire by fire and be roasted to ashes!

13. Father Lord, let Your divine favor and grace bless me and overtake me in every department of my life, in Jesus' name.

14. O God, arise and expose every anti-favor magnet attached to my life. Let them be exposed, disgraced, and destroyed by the fire of God, in Jesus' mighty name.

15. Anointing of fire for directional and locational favor—and blessings that attract destiny helpers—fall upon me now, in the name of Jesus.

16. Father Lord, arise and grant me the divine focus, wisdom, and understanding to achieve total victory in every department of my life, in Jesus' mighty name.

17. Blood of Jesus, pour Your anointing of holy power and grace to achieve what was once too difficult for me. Let Your anointing oil be released upon me now, in the name of Jesus.

18. By the power of the Holy Spirit, I shall possess all of my possessions, in Jesus' mighty name.

19. Every promised land that God has prepared and given to me, I claim you now! I possess you now by fire and by thunder, in the name of Jesus.
20. Blessings that are due to me this season. I command your release! Come upon me now, in the name of Jesus.
21. Every generational curse working against my divine destiny—I command you to break by holy fire and divine thunder, in the mighty name of Jesus Christ!
22. Any generational setback limiting my resources, progress, and promotions, break now and burn to ashes in the name of Jesus.
23. Every anointing and poison of the tail impeding my progress, be cut off and die in the name of Jesus.
24. Every strongman and woman sitting on my glory, I unseat you by fire now, in the name of Jesus.
25. Every dark agent of progress seated at my door of success—waiting to challenge me—receive the slap of fire in the name of Jesus.
26. Any power of darkness using my virtues to trade, return them now, catch fire, and die, in the name of Jesus.
27. Every promise made to me by heaven or anyone in my life that has not materialized, and I call you forth by fire! I call you forth by force, in the mighty name of Jesus.
28. Any and every power holding the keys of my destiny, I command you to release them and expire by fire, in the name of Jesus Christ.

29. My glory, hear my voice! Receive your divine wings and fly to my place of promise in the name of Jesus.
30. Lord, let me be a solution to the problems of kings and dignitaries. Let my name be remembered like Joseph on his way to the palace, in Jesus' mighty name.
31. **John 1:5**: *"And the light shineth in darkness; and the darkness comprehended it not."* Lord, let Your light shine and expel every area of darkness in my life, in the name of Jesus Christ.
32. Power of the living God, release me from spiritual coldness and procrastination that has stagnated my life in the name of Jesus.
33. By the mantle of Elijah, I command every opposing force assigned to hinder my divine elevation to be consumed by holy fire and released from me in the mighty and matchless name of Jesus! Every divine potential lying dormant in me, I command you to arise and shine in the name of Jesus.
34. I break and remove myself from every pattern of promise and failure by the blood of Jesus, in Jesus' mighty name.
35. Father Lord, where I have been disgraced and humiliated, cause men to celebrate me, in Jesus' mighty name.
36. O Lord, expose and disgrace the traps of failure set by unfriendly friends in the name of Jesus.
37. O Lord, let every gift of excellence You've placed in me excel in every department of my life, in Jesus' mighty name.
38. O Lord, anoint me for signs, wonders, and miracles. Let exploits be released upon me now, in the mighty name of Jesus Christ.

39. I command the living Word of God to become breath and life in every area of my life, in the mighty name of Jesus Christ.
40. Fire of the living God, incubate my life with Your power to do all things through Christ who strengthens me.
41. I will arise and shine in every area of my life in the name of Jesus.
42. O Lord, remember me for good, in the name of Jesus.
43. Holy Spirit, distinguish me. Set me apart with Your spirit of excellence and favor in my life, in Jesus' mighty name.
44. I command the grace for unprecedented favor and increase to pursue and overtake my life, in Jesus' mighty name.
45. Holy Spirit, cause me to overtake, expand, and increase in every area of my life, in the mighty name of Jesus Christ.
46. Attacks from the past are making it difficult for me to move forward in my life. Your time is up! Expire by fire and burn to ashes, in Jesus' name.
47. I receive the divine grace to obey the instructions of God's will in the name of Jesus.
48. Lord, make my feet like hind's feet, giving me the stability to dwell in my high places, in Jesus' name.
49. O Lord, pour Your anointing oil of power and favor upon my head, hands, and legs. Let my limbs move my destiny forward by the power in the blood of Jesus Christ.
50. I plead the blood of Jesus over my mind, body, spirit, soul, and every area of my life, in Jesus' name.
51. I thank You, Father, for answered prayers, in Jesus' name.

Closing Prayer

Heavenly Father,

I lift up before You the works of our hands, our tears, and the aspirations of our hearts. I thank You for seeing our efforts and knowing the purity of our hearts in this act of obedience. I trust that as we bring all that we are to You, you will remain faithful. You will honor our faithfulness in return and bless the desires of our hearts according to Your will.

As Your Word declares in **Ecclesiastes 7:8**, *"The end of a matter is better than its beginning,"* we thank You for bringing us to this point of completion. I know that Your plan for me is greater than I could ever imagine. May the seeds I have sown bear fruit in Your perfect timing.

Father, Your Word also encourages me in **Isaiah 60:1**, *"Arise, shine, for your light has come, and the glory of the Lord rises upon you."* I declare that we are rising in this season, stepping boldly into the fullness of all You have called me to possess. I possess my possessions, and I walk in the light and glory that You have set before me.

Lord, I thank You for the support You have provided, and I ask that You continue to bless each one on their journey. May You answer every prayer with unfiltered joy and abundant blessings. May Your peace surround me, and may I walk forward in Your grace and favor, knowing that I have been called to arise and shine for Your glory.

In Jesus' mighty name, we pray, Amen.

Faith Confession Prayer Glossary

1. Prayer Against Addiction

Lord, according to **Psalm 91:2**, I declare that You are my refuge and fortress. I take refuge in Your presence and ask for deliverance from every form of addiction that holds me captive. Break the chains of dependency, Lord, and set me free. I declare, as Your Word in **Isaiah 54:17** says, *no weapon formed against me shall prosper*. Addiction will not have the final say over my life. Amen.

2. Prayer for Deliverance from Depression

Heavenly Father, I come under Your shelter, for You are my refuge. As stated in **Psalm 91:4**, *cover me with Your feathers and give me peace*. I ask for Your light to penetrate the darkness of depression. Your Word in **Isaiah 54:10** says that your unfailing love will not be shaken. I cling to that promise, believing that You will lift my spirit and restore my joy. Amen.

3. Prayer Against Anxiety

Lord God, according to **Psalm 91:5**, *I will not fear the terror of the night nor the arrow that flies by day*. You have promised to be with me, and I declare that anxiety has no hold over my mind. In **Isaiah 54:14**, Your Word says, *"In righteousness, you will be established; tyranny will be far from you; you* *will have nothing to fear."* I speak peace over my thoughts and rest in Your protection. Amen.

4. Prayer for Healing from Deadly Infirmity

Father, in the mighty name of Jesus, I declare the promises of **Psalm 91:16** over my life: *"With long life, I will satisfy him and show him my salvation."* I speak healing over my body, mind, and soul. By Your stripes, I am healed. According to **Isaiah 54:17**, no deadly infirmity will prevail against me. I receive complete healing and restoration. Amen.

5. Prayer of Protection from Evil

Lord, according to **Psalm 91:3**, *You will deliver me from the snare of the fowler and from the deadly pestilence.* I stand firm in Your promise of protection and ask that You shield me from every attack against my well-being. Let Your Word in **Isaiah 54:17** prevail, that *no weapon formed against me shall prosper.* Cover me, Lord, under the shadow of Your wings. Amen.

6. Prayer for Mental Clarity and Strength

Father God, I pray for mental clarity and strength, declaring **Psalm 91:11**: *"For He will command His angels concerning you to guard you in all your ways."* Remove the fog of confusion, anxiety, and depression from my mind. As **Isaiah 54:10** declares, your covenant of peace will never be removed. Let my mind be renewed in Your truth. Amen.

7. Prayer Against Fear and Panic

Lord, I declare that I will not be afraid, for You are with me. According to **Psalm 91:5**, *I refuse to fear any terror by night or arrow by day*. I speak peace over my heart, and I rebuke every spirit of panic and fear. **Isaiah 54:14** says *I will be established in righteousness, and I will be far from oppression*. I receive Your peace, Lord. Amen.

8. Prayer for Emotional Healing

Father, you are my healer. According to **Psalm 91:14**, *You will deliver those who set their love upon You*. Heal my broken heart and bind up my wounds. I pray for emotional healing from past hurts and declare **Isaiah 54:10** that *your unfailing love will not be removed from me*. Let me walk in wholeness. Amen.

9. Prayer for Freedom from Bondage

Lord, I stand on Your Word in **Psalm 91:7**: *"A thousand may fall at your side, ten thousand at your right hand, but it will not come near you."* I pray for freedom from every bondage, addiction, and destructive behavior. **Isaiah 54:17** assures me that *no weapon formed against me will succeed*. I am set free by Your power. Amen.

10. Prayer for Physical Healing and Strength

Heavenly Father, I claim the promise of **Psalm 91:9-10**, that *no harm will overtake me, no disaster will come near my tent*. I pray for physical healing and strength over my body. According to **Isaiah 54:17**, no sickness will prevail against me. Strengthen me, Lord, and restore my health completely. Amen.

11. Prayer for Peace Amidst Chaos

Lord, you are my refuge and my fortress, as **Psalm 91:2** declares. In the midst of chaos and anxiety, I seek Your peace. Let Your peace, which surpasses all understanding, guard my heart and mind. **Isaiah 54:10** reminds me that *Your peace covenant stands firm*. I receive Your calming presence now. Amen.

12. Prayer for Rest and Restoration

Father God, I declare that I find rest under Your wings, as promised in **Psalm 91:4**. Restore my soul, mind, and body from the weariness of life. I declare, as in **Isaiah 54:17**, that *no weapon formed against me will succeed*. Bring me to a place of peace and restoration. Amen.

www.ingramcontent.com/pod-product-compliance
Lightning Source LLC
Chambersburg PA
CBHW060802050426
42449CB00008B/1492